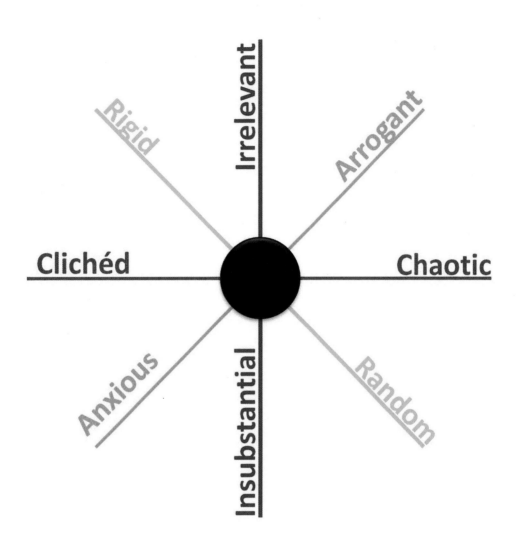

Centered Presentations

Jennifer Palus

Table of Contents

Dedicated to all those who put their hearts and souls into presentations and wonder if it matters. It does.

Foreword by Tom Searcy

The silver bullet sales presentation is a legend of American business. TV shows from *Bewitched* to *Mad Men* celebrate the image of a compelling presentation offered by a dynamic presenter to a jaded, small audience of executives. As the insights unfold, the reserved attendees lean forward, and the final miracle idea is revealed over the crescendo of the buyers shouting "Let's do it!"

What a great piece of nostalgic time-capsule Americana. That's right; tuck it away with your Saturday Evening Post covers painted by Norman Rockwell and the whistle soundtrack from The Andy Griffith Show, because it is a part of the past, not to be repeated.

The reality of the modern presentation is different than Hollywood. Today, the presentation scenario is less of a performance and more of a conversation. It is a dialogue between knowledgeable participants who are sharing ideas and potential solutions, rather than a well-rehearsed monologue in a tiny community theater. The element of the dramatic is still present, but along side is the deep need for preparation and intention.

In my own work with hundreds of sales teams preparing presentations, the focus is often on creating an effective balance. As teams present their solutions to complex problems in complex marketplaces, achieving the right mix of tone, elements and ideas is a challenge.

I am excited about this book because it gives a framework for creating not only better presentation documents, but better presentations. The core components of strategy, balance and presentation materials are all covered in a masterful way with the correct intention: to generate the best opportunity for your company to have its truth heard.

So often, I have seen presenters succumb to the desire to use the most technically advanced presentation tools and displays or to have the cleverest message. They forget the value of striking just the right note in a presentation and lose the opportunity to truly connect with their prospect.

Ernest Hemingway is famous for saying, "I live my life to write one true sentence." Your *truth* in a presentation surpasses the words, images and even interactions.

This book is for a new generation of buyers and presenters. It is about creating in a presentation a chance for connection that shares the pure truth of your company's value with a prospective buyer in such a way that you are truly heard.

Tom Searcy
Founder, Hunt Big Sales

Introduction

The lights dim. The first slide is projected onto the screen. The audience turns its collective attention to the front of the room. The speaker takes a deep breath.

Whether you are the speaker or waiting to watch the presentation the same thought ripples across your mind: ***"Will this be worth my time?"***

Sadly and all too often, the answer is "no."

> Who hasn't sat through a presentation that meandered from idea to idea and never reached a conclusion?

> Haven't you felt your pulse begin to race in sympathy with a presenter whose nerves have taken over?

> How often have you watched brilliant colleagues struggle to make a connection or simply fail to get out of their own way?

> Perhaps you have distracted yourself from vapid narrative by counting the punctuation and grammatical errors in a seemingly random collection of slides.

> How often have you squinted or cringed at slide content obscured by poor choice of color and graphic elements?

I can feel you nodding. And while you're remembering all those weak examples, add to the tally the times when <u>you</u> were the hapless presenter responsible for bringing a less-than-stellar product to your audience. I can almost see your sheepish grin, and it matches the one on my face.

What leads otherwise intelligent, thoughtful, and insightful minds (such as yours and mine) to create and present material that falls short of the mark? Why do we find ourselves or our colleagues wasting compelling content by burying it amid a torrent of distracting and useless discussion?

Over the years, I've come to understand that if you strip away all the variables, you're left with two likely failure points: the material and the delivery.

	Weak Material	Acceptable Material	Strong Material
Strong Delivery	Frustrating	Charismatic	Successful
Acceptable Delivery	Distracting	Commonplace	Latent
Weak Delivery	Cringe-Worthy	Ineffective	Wasted

Combine strong material with strong delivery, and you have the Holy Grail of presentations: well-paced, intriguing, and compelling. The presentation is so well conceived and rehearsed that it appears the presenter is making it up on the spot. There is a dramatic arc to the presentation that draws the audience along to the desired conclusion. Unfortunately, this marriage of delivery and material is the exception rather than the rule.

Even when working with merely acceptable material, a presenter with strong delivery skills can often transform it with the strength of his or her charisma. But even the most effective presenter will flounder when attempting to deliver weak material. Weak content creates an insurmountable obstacle to effective communication, frustrating presenter and audience alike.

The most commonplace presentation is an average presenter using acceptable delivery skills to convey acceptable material. You've no doubt sat through dozens or hundreds of these, let's just say, *adequate* presentations. You might have even recognized how close-to-greatness a particular presentation actually was. Perhaps a little more rehearsal; maybe fewer typos; if only the conclusion was *that* much clearer.

Occasionally, an average, acceptable presenter will have the opportunity to present strong material. The audience often recognizes the latent value of the presentation, and they accept the presenter's limited delivery skill because of the strength of the content.

But the audience will rarely overlook weak material delivery by an average or weak presenter. Even if the presenter has acceptable delivery skills, the audience becomes distracted by content that is confusing, cluttered, inaccurate, or incomplete. Combine weak content with truly weak delivery, and the result is a cringe-worthy presentation, memorable for all the wrong reasons.

Just as a strong presenter can sometimes overcome weak material, you may find a presentation with content so compelling that it can withstand the weakest delivery. But more likely, the meeting will begin to sag under the weight of weak delivery, and the entire presentation will be deemed a failure. The ideas are ignored. The sale lost. The presentation wasted.

So, how do you move from weak to strong? It's not enough to hope that next time will be "better." You need to find the root cause rather than focus on the symptom.

	Weak Material	Acceptable Material	Strong Material
Strong Delivery			
Acceptable Delivery			
Weak Delivery			

This book is designed to help you:

- Determine if you, or members of your team, are out of balance along four presentation dimensions.
- Understand what it means to be centered along the dimensions and the best practices in each.
- Develop an action plan for the specific areas where you can increase the effectiveness of your material and/or delivery.
- Create a shared vocabulary within your team that will enable and encourage professional feedback.

Note: I use the term "slides" throughout the book since PowerPoint is such a common presentation tool; however, the advice applies to any method or media.

The Dimensions of Presentation

Leo Tolstoy wrote, "Happy families are all alike; every unhappy family is unhappy in its own way." When you see a good presentation, you are more focused on the <u>message</u> than the content or the delivery. But when you witness a train wreck of a presentation, you become very aware of the flaws in the material and the delivery.

Every bad presentation has unique factors that limit its effectiveness, but there are definite categories to consider when assessing what went wrong and how to address the issues in the future. Simply stated, a weak presentation will have missed the mark on one or more of these four key dimensions:

Content

Creative

Conversation

Confidence

Content

Content refers to all the information you choose to include in your presentation, whether printed on a slide or spoken. When tasked with building a new presentation, most of us think about _content_ first: what to say and how to say it.

If your grade and high school experience was like mine, you were taught how to build outlines with logical hierarchies, paragraphs with topic sentences, and reports with a structured flow. And, no doubt, these skills have served you well in the business world. The downside of this academic approach to content is that it focuses on HOW we are communicating rather than WHAT we need to say.

We generate stronger content when we consider the HOW only after we determine the WHAT. By making clear decisions about what our audience needs to understand, we create a filter that informs decisions about what to include.

The challenge is to identify the right mix of facts, anecdotes, statistics, and diagrams that make your point without including any more than your audience needs.

When content is balanced it is incisive. When it is out of balance it becomes insubstantial or irrelevant.

Content may be an issue for you or your team if you routinely find:

- You are unable to present all your slides in the allotted time.
- Your presentation falls far short of the expected duration.
- Your audience derails your agenda, focusing on other topics.
- Your audience does not seem to grasp the concepts in your presentation or the desired next steps.

Creative

In the context of presentations, **creative** is used as a noun rather than an adjective. "The creative" refers to the templates, graphics, colors, photography, clipart, fonts and every element that creates the look and feel of a presentation.

Years ago, there were only a few delivery mechanisms for content; most of them were print. The average person was familiar with books, newspapers, magazines, and brochures. These were the de facto templates for business communication as well. Today's audience is comfortable with dozens of communication methods and media, from terse tweets to intuitive infographics to animated websites.

Now, let me be clear: most business presentations do not need to be state-of-the-art multimedia extravaganzas. In fact, with rare exception, a presentation that has too many bells and whistles will raise the eyebrows of your prospect as he wonders, "What are they hiding?" I'm not suggesting you need a team of Disney Imagineers to develop your next presentation. Rather, you need to be cognizant of the experience and expectations of your audience and leverage your creative tools to make your presentation as interesting and compelling as possible.

When we develop presentation materials, we must find a balance between the need to engage our audience and the need to reinforce our company's brand and communication guidelines.

Signs that may point to an issue within your **creative**:

- Your audience visibly winces at the color combinations or animation.
- If you lose your place when presenting, it's hard to get back on track because every slide looks essentially the same.
- Although you try not to, you find yourself reading your text-heavy slides to your audience.
- You avoid sharing your presentation with your internal brand team.

Conversation

The conversation dimension includes how you organize your presentation, how you move from topic to topic, and how you engage with the audience. In the case of a more formal presentation, this includes how you build audience rapport and interact during questions. In more intimate meetings, the conversation is more of a dialogue than monologue.

Presenting with a relaxed, likable conversational tone takes practice and planning. The irony is that those who appear most at ease, most natural, are often the most prepared and rehearsed.

Think of an excellent stage play. The actors appear to be living in the scene, thinking of their words as they go, just like real life. If you are at a play where it's obvious the actors are delivering memorized lines, the magic of theater disappears. Actors strive for "rehearsed spontaneity," and this is also the key to strong presentation delivery.

As effective presenters, we need to consider the arc of the meeting as a conversation, planning give and take with our audience. Conversation is difficult when your approach is too rigid or when you present a flow of ideas that appears random.

You or your team may need to focus on conversation if:

- You are doing almost all the talking in your meetings.
- You shut down conversation in order to stay on your planned timing.
- You realize you've been talking for ten minutes about a topic that is not covered in your presentation content.
- You think of your major point as a big "reveal" and don't want to give anything away until you get there.
- You avoid rehearsal so that you will sound natural; you wing it.

Confidence

As the old joke goes, more people are afraid of public speaking than are afraid of dying. So, they would rather be <u>in</u> the casket at a funeral than giving the eulogy.

There's no denying that getting up in front of an audience of strangers and peers can be intimidating. Most of us feel exposed and judged. And, make no mistake, we <u>are</u> exposed and we <u>are</u> judged in that situation.

The audience is making critical judgments about our competence based on how well we convey expertise while appearing neither arrogant nor uncertain. And that is the dimension of confidence.

Whether you believe that your confidence level is a learned attribute or predetermined like the color of your eyes, there are specific behaviors that convey confidence. As presenters, we use these behaviors to increase the likelihood that we are <u>perceived</u> as confident, regardless of how we feel.

Of course, many people find that when they assume a confident air, they actually begin to feel more confident. The converse is true: we can make ourselves feel more nervous and unsure by focusing on our anxieties.

This is not a self-help book, so the underlying truth of your confidence is not on the table. Instead, we will explore how a strong presenter can understand how he is perceived and work to center this dimension.

Signs you may have a perceived confidence issue

- Audience members have told you they could not hear or understand you.
- You rarely get questions from your audience.
- Audience members direct questions to other members of your team.
- You find yourself tongued-tied when asked to clarify a slide topic.
- You hear yourself, but cannot stop, using "um" in every sentence.

You may have noticed that two of these dimensions are about the material: **CONTENT** and **CREATIVE**. The other two focus on the delivery: CONVERSATION and CONFIDENCE.

Understanding where you have room for improvement is an important step. The chapters that follow will explain each dimension, offer an assessment tool to determine your tendencies, and explore the behaviors and attributes of a centered presentation, as well as the risks of drifting from the center.

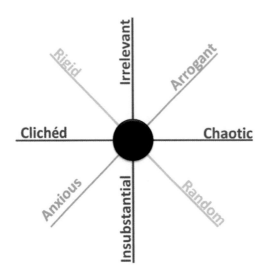

Interestingly, if we get negative feedback about a presentation and acknowledge we need to improve, we sometime overcompensate. It's human nature to want to stay in our comfort zone; to try to fix a problem with MORE of what we're good at. But when it comes to these critical dimensions, you have to be careful, because MORE can quickly become TOO MUCH and push you off center.

Content

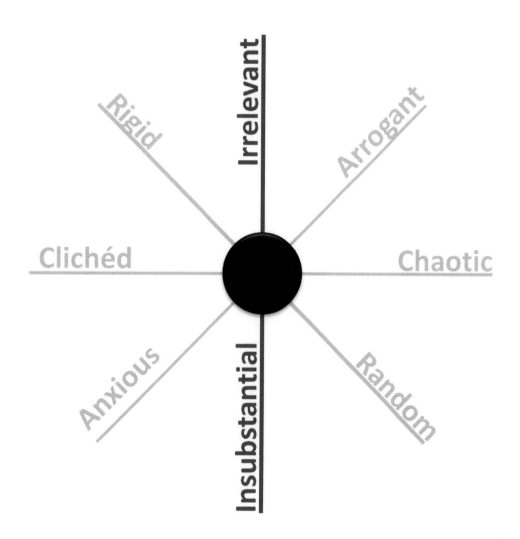

Content Dimension

When someone asks you "how's that presentation coming?" they are usually referring to the material you will include in the slides. Of course, the material on the page/screen is only one component of the full presentation. And that is an important distinction.

When we create the material for a presentation, we are not writing a book, a memo, or a blog; we are creating the material that will support, illustrate, and augment the *narrative* that the presenter will deliver.

Just as a presenter might feel a bit exposed presenting without her slides, the content should feel a bit incomplete without the voice-over that brings it to life.

> **Because it is designed to be *presented*, your presentation does not and should not stand alone.**

The corollary to this rule is that the presentation is there for the audience not for the presenter. Please don't build your slides with an eye to what you (or another presenter) want to remember when the slides are presented. PowerPoint is not a teleprompter.

> **Your slides should contain what the audience needs to know, not what the presenter needs to know.**

Content Definitions

A centered presentation contains *incisive* content: material that is clear and direct. The material conveys a distinct point of view with enough facts, analysis and references to support the presenter's opinions and conclusions. The content does not get bogged down in detailed tangents or academic arguments.

A presentation can drift away from the center of the content dimension by not have a clear voice or by offering too much opinion and not enough fact. This type of content is too *insubstantial* to persuade your audience.

On the other hand, a presentation that includes too many facts is perceived as confusing and *irrelevant*. When material attempts to provide a comprehensive view of a topic, it often ends up conveying too many facts and not enough opinions or conclusions.

Insubstantial   Incisive   Irrelevant

Where do you stand on this dimension? Do you have a feeling or have you received feedback that lets you plot yourself on the continuum? If not, the next page has a brief quiz that can help you assess how centered your presentations are in terms of content.

Avoid selecting the answer that you think is "right." Rather, try to assess what you have done in the past. You might also ask your co-workers, boss, or a client to assess your approach to presentation content.

Content Quiz

1) Prior to your meeting, the prospect says she is only interested in one of your five products. Your response?
    a) Delete all slides that refer to other products to streamline your meeting.
    b) Retain the product family overview but move detail of the other four to an appendix.
    c) Use the full presentation and explain each product in detail; she might be mistaken.

2) Do you do any research for a meeting with a new prospect in your industry?
    a) Not usually; for a first meeting, the existing deck effectively covers the details; research can come later.
    b) Maybe; I try to review the trades and websites for current references to use in my voice-over to freshen the existing deck.
    c) Yes; I would include several new slides on recent trends; I believe that part of proving our credentials is showing we really know the industry.

3) In general, your bullet points:
    a) List/describe topics, i.e., the word or phrase is a noun.
    b) List/describe actions, i.e., the phrase begins with a verb.
    c) Provide a complete narrative, i.e., the bullet is a paragraph.

4) Do you provide the source of external facts and quotes used in a presentation?
    a) I rarely use external information.
    b) I include the link or source as a footnote of the slide.
    c) I include the full source in an appendix and a separate bibliography slide.

5) You spot a relevant article on the plane going to your meeting, do you:
   a) Scan it for context, but don't change the presentation this close to meeting?
   b) Distill a key idea and make note to use in voice-over during presentation?
   c) Use your smartphone to snap a picture of the article and quickly generate a new slide?

6) Your rehearsal timed out at 60 minutes for a 45 minute presentation; the analysis section is too long, so
   a) You delete all the math slides and focus on the conclusions.
   b) You create a slide that shows thumbnails of the analysis and put detailed slides into a leave-behind.
   c) You call the client to add 15 minutes to your meeting.

7) Your client's boss missed the meeting and wants to be brought up to speed via email; you
   a) Explain your presentation requires <u>you</u> to bring it to life and schedule a repeat visit.
   b) Provide a Word document that outlines your key points in 1-2 pages.
   c) Send the presentation deck as an attachment in a reply email.

8) In general, are you more likely to differentiate your company from your competitors by
   a) Using words like "value," "quality," and "partner."
   b) Demonstrating results with case studies.
   c) Providing detailed analysis of relative strengths and weaknesses.

9) Your engineering department provided a complex diagram with animated builds, but they cannot attend an initial pitch meeting, so you
   a) Show the full diagram and attempt to provide a quick overview.
   b) Show the full diagram, and then zoom-in on 2-3 specific sections to highlight important topics.
   c) Build the diagram from beginning to end, have engineer on speaker phone for questions.

10) How would you like your audience to feel after your presentation?
    a) Intrigued
    b) Informed
    c) Impressed

Scoring

1 point for each A	1
5 points for each B	35
10 points for each C	20
Total Score	56

Content	Insubstantial	Incisive	Irrelevant
	10-35 Points	36-65 Points	66-100 Points
Your Score		56	

Does your score feel accurate? Would your audience agree? Does your content sometimes drift away from the center to one of the less effective ends of the continuum?

Centering Content

Interestingly, when presenters feel themselves or the presentation start to wobble, they often try to correct the situation by adding MORE of what they are comfortable with. So someone who is comfortable with facts and research may throw in <u>more</u> when she feels the material isn't quite working.

But the key to finding balance in your presentation is to counteract your natural tendencies and leave your comfort zone.

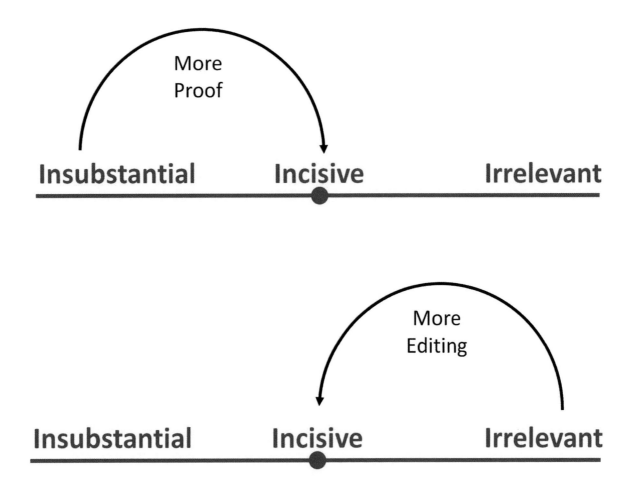

Insubstantial Content

We can't always put our finger on exactly why a presentation feels insubstantial, but somehow the content does not feel adequate or accurate. There are several common elements that lead us to this conclusion:

No Point of View

Every member of your audience is busy and could easily find at least five other things to do in the time they are investing in your presentation. The presentation needs to hold their attention and make it very clear why they are here, what they will learn, what you want them to do, and what happens next. When the presentation is vague on any of these points, the audience disengages. They are physically in the room, but you've lost them.

No Reason to Believe

Business presentations are usually trying to persuade, not just inform. You're selling something, even if it is an idea rather than a product or service. As such, your presentation needs to identify a need and promise to meet it. But you can't just make the promise; you have to back it up. The most common reason a presentation is perceived as insubstantial is because it does not give the audience a reason to believe.

A Reason to Question

Contrast a presentation with no reason to believe with a presentation that gives the audience dozens of tiny reasons to question its accuracy. Audiences are distracted by small typos, formatting issues such as inconsistent use of capitalization, and errors in calculations. We are all human, and we understand how easy it is to make a mistake. At the same time, each mistake is a chink in the armor of the logic of the presentation. If you can't run spell-check, the audience may wonder, can you handle my business?

Insubstantial Example

Company Overview

- World-class inferstructure
- A Bias For Action And A Passion For Results
- Unflagging adherence to the highest standards of business conduct
- Principle-centered solutions to meet our customers' needs
- A portfolio of brands to differentiate our offering and leverage our platforms

At first glance, they look similar, but the slide above is filled with buzzwords and vague concepts. It does not answer the audience's question, "Why do I care?" It also has a typo in the first bullet and inconsistent capitalization on the second; small errors like this can distract your audience and weaken your message.

The slide below focuses on proof points and also highlights the most important idea in a clear way.

Incisive Example

Company Overview

- New clients consistently reduce their costs by 20-40% in their first year with us
- Our global network of offices enables 24/7 phone support and fast turn-around
- Recognized by Forrester as a "company to watch" in 2010 and 2012
- We invest 15% of each year's revenue in research and development

Over 80% of our clients were referred by an existing client

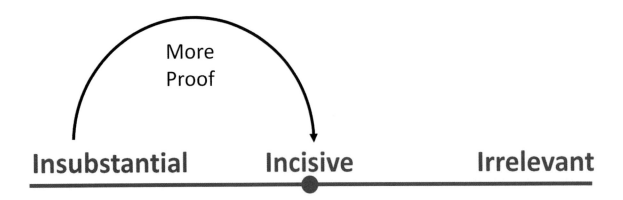

If you tend toward insubstantial content, you need to find ways to incorporate more proof points in your presentation. You need to ground your opinions, check your facts (and spelling), and you need to be sure to have a clear point-of-view. Here are some tips to move your presentation toward the center.

1. **Know What You Believe.** Don't be wishy-washy. Establish your point-of-view (POV) and write it on a big sheet of paper as you build your presentation. Make the content echo your POV.

2. **Get Specific.** Avoid language that could easily be applied to your competitors or a company in a different industry. Words like "quality" and "value" are hollow if you don't back them up.

3. **Prove It.** Count <u>every</u> claim you make in the presentation; (e.g., "We can save you up to 20%," "Our clients are satisfied"). Are you making too many? Do you include an external proof point (fact or anecdote) for each? Will your audience believe you? Strive to include only claims you can convey with confidence and proof.

4. **Proof the Proof.** Be sure to have your presentation proofread by someone else; it's nearly impossible to find all of your own errors.

5. **Shout it out.** Include callouts that give your conclusions. Overtly demonstrate "this is important to you [audience] because…" Don't be afraid to make conclusions and lead the audience to them. But please avoid exclamation points – they actually weaken your message.

Irrelevant Content

An audience needs to understand your argument and follow your logic. They want enough information but not too much. When you give them MORE than they need, the content is perceived as irrelevant. There are several variations:

Drinking from a Fire Hose

With the best of intentions, some presentations pepper the audience with an unrelenting array of facts. The audience may, in fact, have wanted and needed the information, but when it is too fast, too dense, or simply too much, they cannot absorb it. The goal is not to tell the audience everything *you* know; rather to tell them what they *need* to know.

Selling Past the Close

When a salesperson keeps explaining his product after the customer has said yes, that's called "selling past the close." Presenters can fall into the same trap. Imagine you found several different ways to explain something, and rather than pick the best you left all three in the presentation. This issue can also arise if your presentation is poorly organized, and content that belongs in section A is inserted in section C. In this case there's nothing inherently wrong with the specific content, but it becomes irrelevant because it is not presented in the correct context.

SQUIRREL!!

Sometimes a presentation is perceived as irrelevant because its content is, in fact, <u>not</u> relevant. As you are building a presentation, especially if you work with a team, you will cycle through different ideas. There will be iterations and blind alleys on the path to your final product. Make sure you don't leave remnants of abandoned ideas within your presentation.

The slide above has too many ideas and too much detail. Some of the ideas need to be edited down; others need to be deleted or moved to a more appropriate slide.

Incisive Example

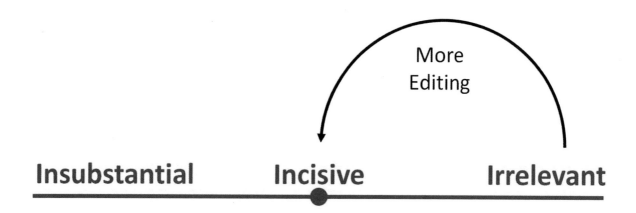

Insubstantial   **Incisive**   **Irrelevant**

If you feel (or have been told) that you drift toward irrelevant content, then you need to spend more time editing before you present. Here are some tips:

1. **Stick to One Big Idea.** What do you want the audience to think or do at the end of your presentation? Write it out and use it as a filter for all of your content.

2. **Connect the Dots.** Print out your content and identify the "so what" of every slide. Color-code each element in the deck that draws a straight-line to your big idea.

3. **Be Ruthless.** Set aside all the content that does not directly support your big idea. Now bring back 1-2 of your favorite elements to give the presentation interest. Cut the rest.

4. **Save Your Scraps.** You probably will have to edit out GREAT content – it's just not great for <u>this</u> presentation. Save the content you edit out in logical topic folders, so you can use it where it will serve you better.

Incisive Content

There is, of course, no absolute measure of the correct content for a presentation. Each presentation has a unique combination of background, goal, and audience. We need to align our content appropriately.

A slide about your new software platform that was perfectly relevant for senior level marketing executives would likely feel insubstantial to an audience of technical programmers. An HR presentation that included detailed, accurate and valuable information on selling stock options would feel irrelevant to employees who do not receive that benefit.

While there is no one "right answer" for how to create incisive content, there are several touchpoints in each presentation that you can and should review to be sure your content is as clear and compelling as possible.

- Agenda
- Purpose/Outcome
- Quotes/Claims
- Volume of Content
- Individual Bullets
- "You Are Here" Element
- Headlines
- Recap/Summary
- Next Steps
- Point of View

Agenda

The presence of an agenda provides substance to your presentation; it is a subtle way to show that you have thought about the presentation, its goals, the available time, etc.

- **Incisive**: Agenda with key topics, time blocks, and speakers
- **Insubstantial**: No agenda or only a vague sketch
- **Irrelevant**: A 30 minute meeting with a two-page agenda showing three layers of outlined topics that don't actually align to the subsequent slide content

Purpose/Outcome

I am willing to bet there <u>is</u> a goal for the meeting (if not, please cancel the meeting!), but you might be afraid your goal will be different than the audience's. That's a good problem to have. If you are specific and clear, you <u>and</u> your audience can get on the same page right from the beginning, rather than realizing there was a disconnect after you finish your presentation. Strong presentation content will effectively share the purpose and desired outcomes.

- **Incisive**: Definitive statement of what "success" looks like for the meeting
- **Insubstantial**: No stated goal/purpose/outline or only vague language
- **Irrelevant**: Wordy, overly complicated, overly ambitious

29

Quotes/Claims

If you are referencing others' research or making claims about your success, you need to be able to support your facts, but you don't need to bury the audience in details.

- **Incisive**: Share the relevant quote or metric and include appropriate footnotes and appendices to allow an interested audience member to review or confirm
- **Insubstantial**: Pure copy-paste from websites with no sources (a.k.a. plagiarism) and hyperbolic claims of success with no proof
- **Irrelevant**: Every claim includes a "deep-dive" into the reference material

Volume of Content

This attribute depends very much on the specific meeting: does it *feel* like the right amount. Imagine five department heads presenting at an internal meeting. One manager has 100 slides, while the others have 20. It's <u>possible</u> the long presentation will be fantastic, but strictly based on volume of slides it will probably stray off-topic.

- **Incisive**: An appropriate number of slides for the time and topic
- **Insubstantial**: Too little material; presenter uses < 30% of allotted time
- **Irrelevant**: An overwhelming amount of material; presenter is unable to finish in allotted time or moves so quickly that audience cannot follow

Individual Bullets

Consider each bullet as a micro-presentation: Does it stand alone? Is it appropriate to the topic and aligned to the goal? Does it have superfluous, unneeded, extra, redundant or unnecessary words (ahem)? Are the length and verb tense of the bullets consistent?

- **Incisive**: Bullets are concise and compelling with parallel structure
- **Insubstantial**: Bullets contain typos, different structures, and fragments
- **Irrelevant**: Bullets include full paragraphs and cumbersome vocabulary

"You Are Here" Element

Give your audience a map so that they understand how you are approaching the subject matter and can follow your logic.

- **Incisive**: Establishes the map and repeats at key milestones in presentation
- **Insubstantial**: Rarely includes a map
- **Irrelevant**: Refers to map constantly, cluttering slide with icons, getting bogged down in the flow of the presentation rather than the content

Headlines

We don't always give a lot of thought to our slide headlines, but they can be a powerful tool. How do you use this prime real estate?

- **Incisive**: Headlines convey key topics/ideas. If you were to "read" a list of only the headlines, you'd get a summary of the presentation.
- **Insubstantial**: Generic and repetitive headlines ("Timing," "About Us") that don't add to the understanding of your content
- **Irrelevant**: Complete, wordy sentences that fight with slide content for message dominance

Recap/Summary

The presentation summary is the bookend of the agenda – did you *tell 'em what you said you were going to tell 'em*? This is also a natural point in the presentation to identify any audience expectations that were not met.

- **Incisive**: Clear summary that echoes agenda
- **Insubstantial**: No summary or vaguely worded
- **Irrelevant**: Verbose summary that introduces new concepts or does not reflect the actual body of the presentation

Next Steps

Each presentation is a point on the journey to your goal; the "next steps" section seeks consensus on who will take the next action or decision. This call-to-action is the "close," even if you are not selling something in this particular meeting.

- **Incisive**: The next steps reflect the purpose/outcome shared at beginning
- **Insubstantial**: No discussion of next steps or vaguely worded
- **Irrelevant**: Disjointed next steps that do not flow organically from presentation

Point of View

Consider the entirety of the presentation; does it effectively present a clear idea?

- **Incisive**: A clear voice and a logical flow of ideas
- **Insubstantial**: An uncertain voice, unwilling to state conclusions
- **Irrelevant**: Multiple points of view create disconnection and distraction

Creative

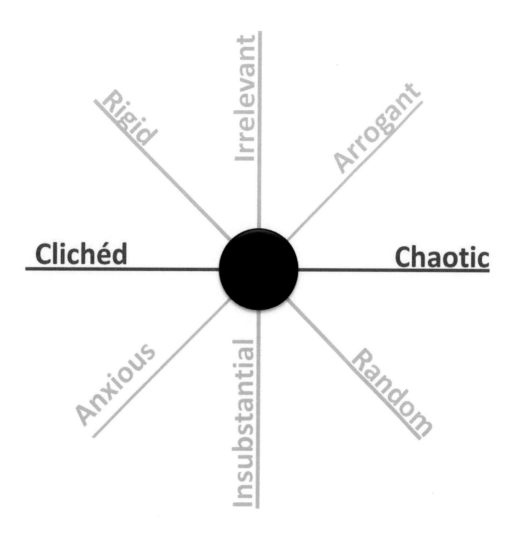

Creative Dimension

There was a time in American business when you would dictate a letter to a secretary to be typed or describe meeting graphics to an artist to be designed and created. Today, most of us type our own emails, and we build all but the most complex presentations ourselves.

This method is more streamlined and efficient, but it can also be less effective if the person doing the design work (that is, us) doesn't have the time, skill, or interest to do a great job. But unless you have the budget to work with a graphic artist, you need to make sure your approach to creative is solid.

> **Follow your company's brand guideline.**
> **If one does not exist, develop your own consistent approach.**

Almost all large companies have a brand guideline; awareness of and respect for these rules will resolve many creative challenges. If you work in a smaller company that has not established a guideline, you can create one for yourself or your team. The consistency it provides will be worth the effort.

The creative includes the slides, handouts, boards, or flipcharts you use to support your narrative. Remember creative is a noun in this context. As stated earlier, I use the term "slides" since PowerPoint is such a common tool; however, the advice applies to any method or media.

Creative Definitions

The goal for a centered presentation is _compelling_ creative that makes your verbal message more understandable, more memorable, and more interesting. In almost every case, the creative should be developed after the content to be sure creative is in a supporting role. (An exception would be if the creative _itself_ is the topic of the presentation.)

When creative causes a presentation's demise, it has shifted from the center in one of two ways.

Clichéd   Compelling   Chaotic

Creative can be decidedly lacking in creativity. Over-used templates, lifeless layouts, predictable clipart are all part of creative that is perceived as _clichéd_.

The other extreme on this dimension is the _chaotic_ presentation, so chock-full of colors, images, and ideas that the message is obscured.

Do you see yourself along this continuum? If not, the quiz on the next page can help you assess your creative dimension.

Creative Quiz

1) How do you incorporate "you are here" elements in your presentation?
   a) I like to repeat the agenda or key topic before each major section.
   b) I try to use a graphic that provides a reference to the presentation flow.
   c) I avoid them, because that lets me change the presentation on the fly.

2) Do you consider your company or client brand guidelines when creating presentations?
   a) Definitely
   b) Sometimes
   c) Rarely

3) Do you use a template for your slide presentations?
   a) Yes, I chose from the template(s) provided by my company or client.
   b) Usually but not always; I know how to modify the template as appropriate.
   c) Rarely, I like the freedom to create a new style with each slide.

4) How do you select colors for your slides, drawings, and graphics?
   a) I type in the RGB formulas on each object to be sure I'm matching brand guidelines.
   b) I create master color palette templates for my company/client.
   c) I pick what looks good from the wheel of colors.

5) How many fonts would you use in an average presentation?
   a) 1-2, usually the ones that are tied to the template.
   b) 2-4, most slides use the template fonts, but I emphasize callouts or objects with additional fonts.
   c) 3-10, fonts break up the monotony of the slide and add interest.

6) Do you know how to manipulate the Slide Master in PowerPoint if needed?
   a) I know where it is, but I prefer to use the templates as provided.
   b) Yes, I sometimes tweak the Slide Master to customize a template.
   c) No. What is a Slide Master?

7) How often do you use clipart and photography?
   a) I rarely use either, less than 20% of my slides have any images.
   b) I like to use one or the other in a presentation; probably 20-60% of my slides have an image.
   c) I use both to make interesting visuals on at least 60% of my slides.

8) Assuming you have no access to a graphic artist to create images, how would you select clipart?
   a) I'd type in words in the PowerPoint tool and find images I like.
   b) I'd search on the Microsoft library to find families of clipart images that work well together.
   c) I'd use Google to search images.

9) Builds, animation, and transitions – what's your take?
   a) They don't belong in a professional presentation.
   b) Builds can be effective to clarify a concept when used sparingly; transitions are distracting.
   c) They bring life to the slides and keep the audience interested.

10) What do you hope the audience thinks about your presentation from a creative perspective?
   a) I hope they are listening to my message not considering my creative.
   b) I hope they find my creative supports and illustrates my message.
   c) I hope they find it memorable.

Scoring

1 point for each A	
5 points for each B	
10 points for each C	
Total Score	

Creative	Clichéd	Compelling	Chaotic
	10-35 Points	36-65 Points	66-100 Points
Your Score			

How do you feel about this score? Have you gotten feedback about creative in the past? Do you think there is room for improvement?

Centering Creative

As mentioned in the content section, the challenge in finding your center is in fighting the natural tendency to do what feels comfortable to you.

Those who provide too much or not enough creative often have the same underlying motivation: they have seen too many presentations that they considered "wild" or "boring," and they went to the other extreme.

As with all of the dimensions of centered presentations, the trick is to avoid the extremes.

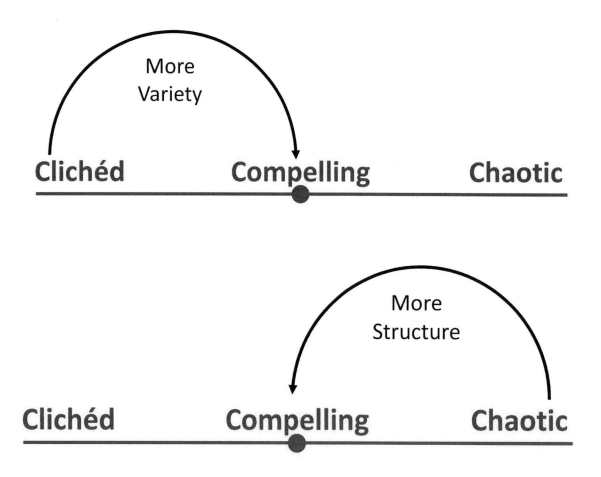

The Clichéd Presentation

An overuse of text-only, bullet slides is the most obvious symptom of clichéd presentations. When graphics are used in this type of presentation, they tend to be recognized as part of the initial PowerPoint clipart set (circa 1993). Three attitudes lead us to create this type of presentation:

I'm Just Not Creative

Somewhere in your early life you discovered you didn't enjoy arts and crafts, or perhaps your efforts were judged harshly by a sibling or teacher. Whatever the cause, you see yourself as "left-brained" and don't like to dabble in the creative side of presentations. Your slides tend to be text-heavy with very limited use of graphics. You don't have to change who you are, but you can partner with more creative colleagues or use some tools and templates that let you present your information with more flair without going overboard.

I Know This Way is Safe

Using the same tried-and-true templates, layouts, colors, clipart, and fonts is a safe choice… but also boring for your audience. Perhaps you just never thought about giving your presentation more variety. Or perhaps you were chastised at some point for being "too creative" or for not following brand guidelines. You tend to find a formula and stick to it. Expanding your repertoire will help you engage with your audience.

I Hate It When Others Get "Creative"

The third attitude that leads us to develop clichéd presentations is an overreaction to having to sit through a chaotic presentation. After we recover from the glaring colors, dazzling animation, and onslaught of clipart, we vow to "never" create <u>anything</u> like that. But as in most things, we need to respond with moderation. Some creative variation is important to an effective presentation.

Text-heavy presentations can shift toward more compelling creative by including simple diagrams, charts, and graphics. Give your audience something more than the clichéd bullet list, and you may also find graphics make your message clearer.

Clichéd Examples

Compelling Examples

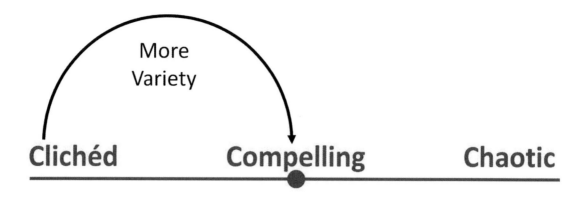

Clichéd   Compelling   Chaotic

If you want to shift from clichéd to compelling creative, your goal is to develop a creative esthetic that is simple but not boring; here are some tips.

1. **Focus on the Ratio.** Use simple ratios or rules of thumb to include a variety of slides. If you rarely use anything beyond the standard bullet list, strive to include at least 20% (and then move up to 40%, then 60%) of slides that have a graphic, chart, or interesting layout.

2. **Get Smart with SmartArt.** PowerPoint includes a library of diagrams that can make a simple bullet list more interesting and dynamic. Don't overuse them (they, too, can become clichéd), but discover how the different shapes and diagrams can be used to convey your ideas.

3. **Use Fewer Words.** Even if you're not comfortable with a lot of images or graphics, trying reducing the number of words on your slides (maybe only include 1 or 2 on a solid background) so that the words themselves feel more graphic and important.

The Chaotic Presentation

Chaotic creative tends to be the result of a lack of editing. It is easier to "tone down" a chaotic presentation than to "liven up" a clichéd presentation. But if you neglect to edit, the net result is the same: your audience will not engage with you or your message. It can be helpful to ask someone outside your team to review your presentation; their fresh eyes will quickly see where your creative is an obstacle to your message. If your presentations fall into this category, you've probably thought:

Never Again

You've sat through too many boring presentations and vowed "never again." You just want to make it interesting for the audience. But if you throw too much into your presentation, your audience becomes distracted. Never forget that the message needs to be more interesting than the packaging.

Maybe This Will Help

Often individual slides include wonderful ways of representing information; clever use of tables, graphics, builds, color-coding can all help the presenter tell a better story. But no matter how strong the individual ideas, they can lead to chaos when there are too many different schemes, metaphors, and constructs mixed together.

More Is . . . More

Some people just LOVE color, movement, and variety. They dress with great style, they decorate their offices with flair, they come up with out-of-the-box solutions, and they are great people to have on a team. If this describes you, be certain when developing a presentation that creative is aligned to your audience. A wildly creative presentation may be perfect for a meeting with a start-up software company but inappropriate when talking to a bank.

When a presentation uses too many colors, too many fonts, a mismatched template, too much clipart, inappropriate humor (e.g. "house of cards" on the schedule below), and illustrations rather than actual facts, the overall impact is chaotic. Simplify and edit to move back toward compelling, centered creative.

Chaotic Examples   **Compelling Examples**

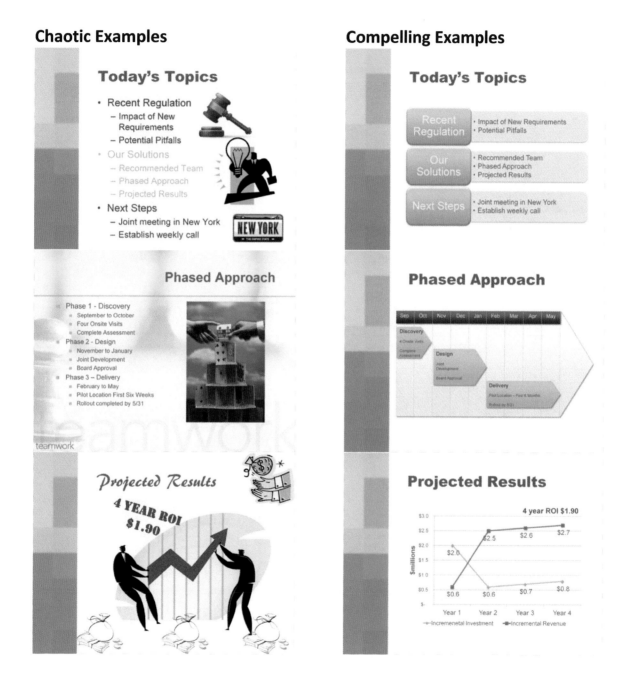

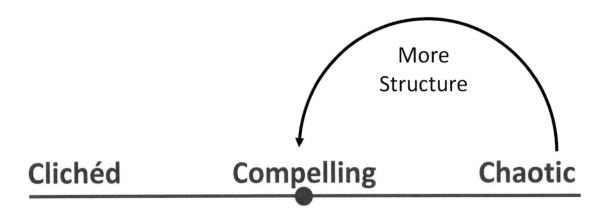

Clichéd **Compelling** **Chaotic**

If you want to move your creative storytelling from a chaotic to compelling approach, here are some suggestions:

1. **De-clutter.** Not counting template/background graphics, do you have more than one graphic element (clipart, image, or chart) on a slide? Delete them unless you are 100% sure they are required to make your point.

2. **Streamline.** In general, avoid using more than two fonts on the same slide, more than one template in the same presentation, or combining clipart and photography on the same slide. There are exceptions, but if you know you tend toward chaotic, it's safer to keep it simple.

3. **Ease Up.** Give the audience a chance to rest their eyes and their brains. Include at least 20% slides that are text-only. Rather than being boring, these slides create a frame and foundation for your more visually-oriented slides.

The Compelling Presentation

When you center the creative elements, you will have a compelling presentation, although as with the content elements, there is no one "right way" to use creative. There are, however, some rules of thumb to consider when developing and fine-tuning your presentation.

- Brand Guideline
- Number of Fonts
- Font Size
- Number of Colors
- Graphics
- Logo Placement
- Slide Layout
- Clipart
- Photography
- Charts

Brand Guideline

If your company or your client has brand guidelines, be sure to use them when building your presentation.

- **Compelling**: Respects guideline but with personality
- **Cliché**: Follows guideline exactly; presentation looks like example
- **Chaotic**: Flagrant violation of brand guidelines

Number of Fonts

When used well, fonts are not noticed by the viewer. When used poorly, they leap out at us. If you combine material from multiple sources, be careful that you do not introduce additional fonts accidentally. It's a good idea to paste foreign content as "unformatted text," so that the content integrates into your existing formatting.

- **Compelling**: Uses a primary font, may add a second or third as accent or to draw attention to callouts
- **Cliché**: Employs a single font, usually Ariel or Times New Roman
- **Chaotic**: Different source material has different fonts; multiple fonts are used in the same graphic element for no apparent reason

Font Size

Readability is the primary concern for font size. Make sure you are not making your audience squint at the screen or at your handouts. If you are presenting on a screen, never use a typeface smaller than 16 point. If you are presenting from handouts, use 12 point or larger. Beyond audience comfort, font size can be used to convey the relative importance of ideas.

- **Compelling**: Planned variation – different sizes in headlines, bullets, and objects to support presentation narrative in a logical way
- **Clichéd**: Standard outline (each bullet slightly smaller)
- **Chaotic**: Random use of different sizes

Number of Colors

If you've ever seen brand guidelines, you know that one of the first topics covered is the color palette. Marketers establish primary colors that convey the emotions and qualities of their brand, along with secondary colors to provide accents. You need to do the same thing with your presentation. If you are using a corporate template, the colors may have already been established; if not, take the time to create a color story.

- **Compelling**: Establishes 2-3 primary colors and then uses 1-2 secondary colors to create interest
- **Clichéd**: Uses the same one or two colors throughout
- **Chaotic**: Random use of five or more colors, sometimes introducing jarring combinations or a not-quite-the-same blue on later slides

Graphics

Presentations are visual media. Slide after slide of text is tedious and makes it harder for the audience to listen. Use graphics to enhance your story and convey in an instant what a block of text cannot.

- **Compelling**: 20% to 60% of slides use graphics; the graphics integrate and support the narrative
- **Clichéd**: Less than 20% of slides include graphics; the graphics are "pasted on" and don't complement the narrative
- **Chaotic**: More than 60% of slides use graphics; the style and placement of graphics is disruptive and distracts from the narrative

Logo Placement

Including your company's logo is literally "branding" your presentation. Because individual slides may become separated from a deck, it is wise to include your logo or company name on all slides.

- **Compelling**: Introduces logo on cover, then use a background position on subsequent slides; logo present but unobtrusive
- **Clichéd**: Missing or only on cover slide
- **Chaotic**: Logo is randomly placed and sized throughout presentation; competes with the graphics that support slide content

Slide Layout

In the 1990's there was only one style of PowerPoint slide. Today there are several variations, and savvy users can also customize their own layouts.

- **Compelling**: Creates a library of 2-3 primary layouts and employs different layouts that support different types of content
- **Clichéd**: Uses only the traditional bullet list slide layout
- **Chaotic**: Uses a wide variety of layouts, often with free-hand (unaligned) borders and elements that vary from slide to slide

Clipart

Clipart can be an effect tool or a distracting element. The goal should be for all graphic elements to look as if they were drawn by the same artist.

- **Compelling**: Uses clipart to support ideas or create iconography with consistent themes and colors

- **Clichéd**: Uses no clipart or ones we've seen hundreds of times

- **Chaotic**: Disjointed approach to clipart, mixing styles, colors, and scale

Photography

Decidedly more "modern" than clipart, photography is very popular in presentations. For the most sophisticated use of photos, you will need photo editing skills (or access to someone who has them). If not, avoid using photography in a way that looks more like a scrapbook than a professional presentation (unless you are in the scrapbook business, of course.)

- **Compelling**: Photography that supports ideas with similar look and feel

- **Clichéd**: No photography or very standard MS Office images

- **Chaotic**: Disjointed approach, with a variety of photography styles; borders and placement distract from slide copy

Charts

Data that seems confusing in a spoken narrative can practically jump off the screen with the right chart.

- **Compelling:** Easy to read charts with a clear, obvious "so what"
- **Clichéd:** Rarely uses charts
- **Chaotic:** Busy charts with complicated legends, multiple axes, and an array of extra bells and whistles that confuse rather than clarify

Presentation Assessment

Review or ask others to review 12-15 slides (a short presentation or subset) and circle the best descriptor in each element:

Content Element	Insubstantial	Incisive	Irrelevant
Agenda	Missing / Light	Aligned to Content	Busy / Disconnected
Purpose / Outcome	Missing / Vague	Clearly Stated	Wordy / Ambitious
Quotes / Claims	Unsupported	Sourced / Footnoted	Fully Detailed
Volume of Content	Skimpy	Appropriate	Overwhelming
Individual Bullets	Ambiguous	Concise	Verbose
"You Are Here" Element	Missing	Periodic Anchor	Constant Reference
Headlines	Generic Phrase	Key Phrase	Full Sentence
Recap / Summary	Missing / Light	Reflects Agenda	Unaligned
Next Steps	Missing / Vague	Reflects Outcome	Unaligned
Point of View	Uncertain	Clear	Several
Score			

Creative Element	Clichéd	Compelling	Chaotic
Brand Guideline	Rigid Adherence	Aligned	Ignored
# of Fonts	1	2-3	4+
Font Size	Standard Outline	Planned Variation	Random
# of Colors	1-2	3-5	5+
Graphics	< 20% Slides	20% - 60% Slides	> 60% Slides
Logo Placement	None or Cover Only	Background	Random
Slide Layout	Primary Bullet List	2-3 Variations	4+ Variations
Clipart	None or "Safe"	Supports Ideas	Disjointed
Photography	None or "Safe"	Supports Ideas	Distracting
Charts	None	Clean / Clear	Busy / Confusing
Score			

Top three items to address:

1.

2.

3.

Where do your presentations normally fall on the chart below?

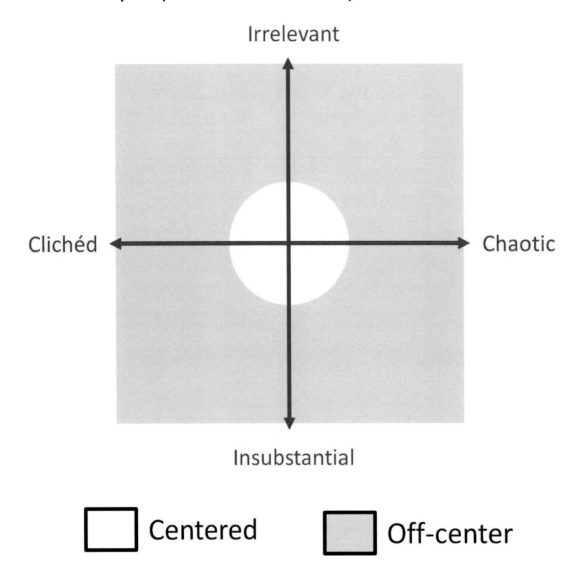

Irrelevant

Clichéd ←——————————→ Chaotic

Insubstantial

☐ Centered   ▨ Off-center

Are you drifting from center?

How do others perceive your presentations?

Content
& Creative

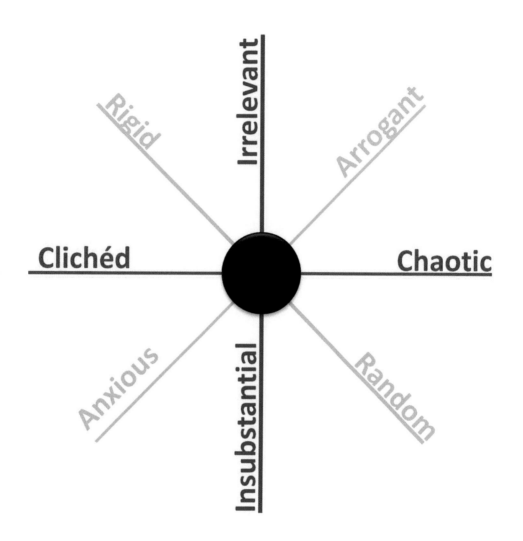

The Intersection of Content and Creative

As mentioned earlier, two of the dimensions of centered presentations are about the material itself: **CONTENT** and **CREATIVE**.

A centered presentation offers incisive content in a compelling way, and the audience finds such a presentation to be <u>**engaging**</u>.

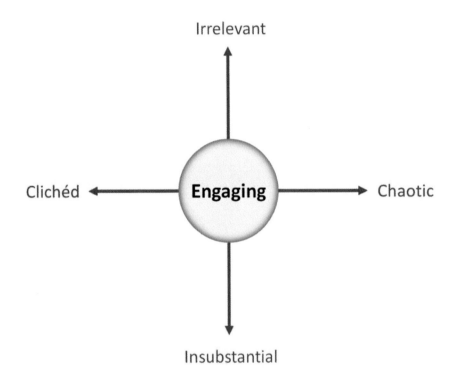

We've talked about how a presentation can drift away from the center along either of these two dimensions. What if a presentation has issues on both dimensions? What happens where content and creative intersect?

Overwhelming Presentations

When irrelevant content is combined with chaotic creative, the resulting presentation is **overwhelming**. There is just too much of everything, and the audience focuses on nothing.

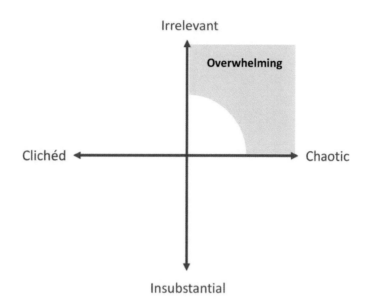

The keys to shift back to center? Editing and structure. If you find your presentations drift from the center into this quadrant, use the checklist below.

- ☐ Have only <u>one</u> big idea for the presentation
- ☐ Include an agenda or table of contents
- ☐ Ruthlessly edit material that is not directly related to the big idea
- ☐ Identify the "so what" of each slide
- ☐ Use overview and summary to ensure audience follows your path

- ☐ Limit to 1-2 fonts
- ☐ Use clipart or photography, not both
- ☐ Limit to 2 primary colors and 2 secondary or accent colors
- ☐ Use build animation on less than 20% of slides
- ☐ Do not use slide transition animation

Boring Presentations

Combine irrelevant content with predicable, clichéd creative and your audience will find it **boring**.

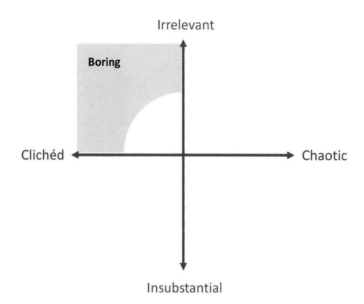

Limit the content to what matters most to your audience and to your big idea. Then add some variety in your creative to maintain their interest. If your presentations tend to be a bit boring, here is a handy checklist:

- ☐ Have only <u>one</u> big idea for the presentation
- ☐ Include an agenda or table of contents
- ☐ Ruthlessly edit material that is not directly related to the big idea
- ☐ Identify the "so what" of each slide
- ☐ Use overview and summary to ensure audience follows your path

- ☐ Strive for 20-40% of slides with graphic objects
- ☐ Use SmartArt to transition from bullet list to graphic
- ☐ Use columns and tables to vary slide layout
- ☐ Use a large photograph or single word to draw attention to an idea
- ☐ Try presenting from a flipchart rather than projecting slides

Distracting Presentations

When insubstantial content is dressed up with chaotic creative elements, the result is **distracting**. The audience may wonder if you are purposely using the creative elements to draw attention away from your lack of facts.

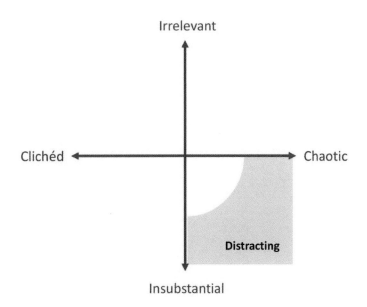

Balance your presentation by adding structure and proof, for example:

- ☐ Identify what the audience should believe and why they should believe
- ☐ Ensure all claims can be supported (on slide or in voice-over)
- ☐ Overtly state your purpose, outcome, and agenda
- ☐ Tie each slide back to your purpose
- ☐ Conclude with a "closing statement" (like on TV) that recaps main points

- ☐ Limit to 1-2 fonts
- ☐ Use clipart or photography, not both
- ☐ Limit to 2 primary colors and 2 secondary or accent colors
- ☐ Use build animation on less than 20% of slides
- ☐ Do not use slide transition animation

Frustrating Presentations

Light, opinion-based content presented in an over-familiar, clichéd way is very **frustrating** for an audience. They wait for a clear argument presented in an interesting way, but it never arrives.

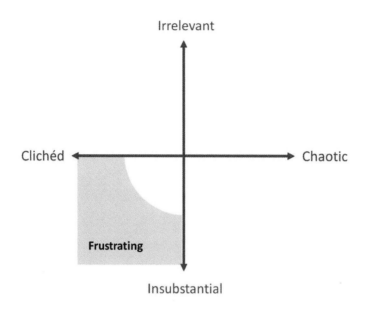

Find ways to incorporate more proof to your content and add variety to your creative to engage the audience. A checklist can help:

- ☐ Identify what the audience should believe and why they should believe
- ☐ Ensure all claims can be supported (on slide or in voice-over)
- ☐ Overtly state your purpose, outcome, and agenda
- ☐ Tie each slide back to your purpose
- ☐ Conclude with a "closing statement" (like on TV) that recaps main points

- ☐ Strive for 20-40% of slides with graphic objects
- ☐ Use SmartArt to transition from bullet list to graphic
- ☐ Use columns and tables to vary slide layout
- ☐ Use a large photograph or single word to draw attention to an idea
- ☐ Try presenting from a flipchart rather than projecting slides

Conversation

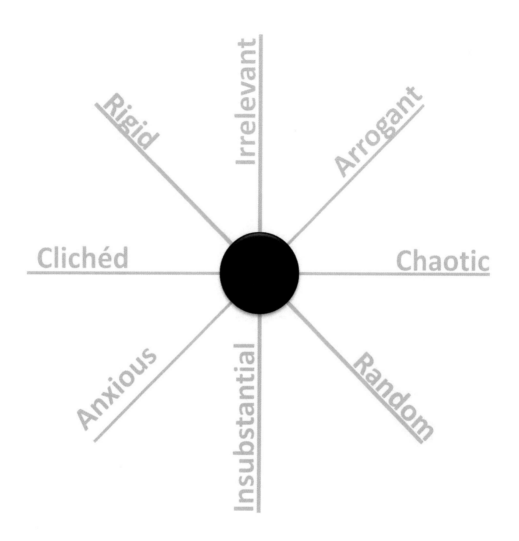

Conversation Dimension

The conversation dimension includes how you organize your presentation, how you move from topic to topic, and if you engage in a dialogue or a monologue.

If you are planning a meeting with a client or prospect, do you consider "the presentation" as a separate block of time from "the discussion"? If so, you might be overlooking the opportunity to increase your interaction during the presentation and to initiate a conversation as you present your material.

When we watch movies or plays, the actors usually pretend there is an invisible "4th wall" between them and the audience or the camera. We are watching the characters interact, but the characters are unaware we are there. There are some exceptions to this: When an actor "breaks the 4th wall" and makes eye contact or talks directly to the audience. I think you'll agree this technique can be tiresome if not used sparingly.

Contrast the theatrical approach with the interactions we have in meetings. Even when we are presenting formally, we are not "acting" for our audience. We are ourselves. And we don't want to establish that artificial barrier of a 4th wall. Not only does it distance you from your audience it also gives them permission to disengage and "just watch."

> Involve your audience to keep them engaged and to ensure you are talking with your audience not at your audience.

Conversation Definitions

A centered presenter engages in _relaxed_ conversation. She has a plan for the meeting, but she is willing to "go off script" if appropriate. She lets her audience be part of the conversation from beginning to end.

Rigid　　　　　　　**Relaxed**　　　　　　　**Random**

When a presenter is not centered, she might be too concerned about the exact flow of content, the timing of the presentation or other "rules." This presenter is perceived as _rigid_.

Move away from center in the opposite direction and you find a presenter whose conversation appears to be _random_. She is so willing to "go with the flow" that the original plan of the meeting is lost.

Do you see yourself in these descriptions? Since it can be hard to judge how we are perceived, you might want to invite a co-worker or client to give you feedback or use the quiz on the next page.

Conversation Quiz

1) Where do you start when building a presentation for a new prospect?
    a) A standard company credential deck that I have used in the past.
    b) A meeting outline based on what I know about the prospect, reusing or building slides as needed.
    c) A blank presentation.

2) About how many slides would you create for a 30 minute meeting with a new prospect?
    a) 15-30, about 30-60 seconds per slide is a good rule of thumb.
    b) No more than 10, to allow time for discussion.
    c) I'd want 40-50 slides with samples and case studies to give them a good overview.

3) Do you rehearse your presentation?
    a) Yes, I even memorize part of it.
    b) Yes, I practice in the mirror and/or with an internal team.
    c) I review it in my head, but I don't like to formally rehearse; it makes it sound canned.

4) Is it helpful to begin the meeting with the purpose or goal for the meeting?
    a) Yes; I always explain why we are there.
    b) Yes; it ensures everyone agrees or allows us to adjust the goal.
    c) No; it's implied. Everyone knows why we are there.

5) How often do you use an agenda or table of contents slide?
    a) Always, it sets the tone and expectations for the meeting.
    b) Usually, though in some settings I might use voice-over or create an agenda with my audience.
    c) Rarely; the conversation needs to be organic and I follow where it leads.

6) Consider a 30-minute meeting with a new prospect, who does most of the talking?
   a) I do about at least 80% of the talking.
   b) I do about 50-75% of the talking.
   c) It really varies; often I just listen and get to know them.

7) When do you use a "parking lot" to capture ideas/topics for later follow-up?
   a) Always, I assign a specific person to be responsible; it keeps us on task.
   b) Yes, if an off-topic discussion will take more than 5% of the meeting, I parking lot it (capture on a flipchart or note pad).
   c) Rarely; I think that if people are interested in a different topic we should explore it.

8) How would you deal with a "sniper" in a meeting (someone who challenges you, a lot)?
   a) I'd answer his questions calmly - then try to ignore him.
   b) I'd invite him to play devil's advocate for the group – using his critical thinking on my terms.
   c) I'd discuss and debate his point of view – that's where the meeting gets interesting.

9) You're stuck in traffic on the way to your meeting, your laptop battery is dead, you have no signal on your smartphone, and you don't have a printout of your presentation. You find a pay phone and . . .
   a) Reschedule the meeting.
   b) Sketch out my main points on a legal pad, call in, and conduct the meeting by phone.
   c) Call my client and get him talking about his kid's soccer game and see where it goes.

10) What one word do you think your presentation style brings to mind for your audience?

   a) Organized
   b) Responsive
   c) Enthusiastic

Scoring

1 point for each A	
5 points for each B	
10 points for each C	
Total Score	

Conversation	Rigid	Relaxed	Random
	10-35 Points	36-65 Points	66-100 Points
Your Score			

Accurately assessing your own conversational style can be difficult, especially in the moment. You might consider, with your audience's permission, recording or videoing a meeting so you can review it later with more objectivity.

Centering Conversation

The pitfalls of this dimension have to do with control – the presenter has drifted from the center when he displays too much control (rigid) or not enough (random).

In both cases, the path back to center is about preparing for the meeting differently.

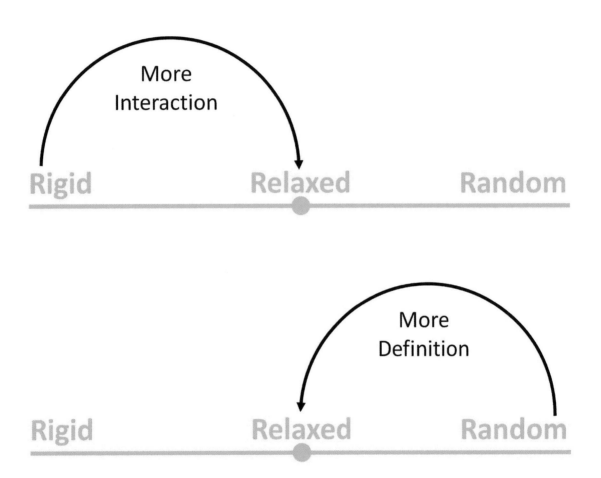

The Rigid Presenter

Rigid presenters often get feedback that their presentations are very good, yet they don't always get the sale or the decision they wanted. That's because the audience didn't engaged in a conversation, perhaps because of one of these attitudes:

I Have a Plan

Many rigid presenters simply over prepare for their presentations. If you fall in this category, you probably imagine every detail from the seating arrangement to the temperature in the room. You rehearsed your talking points, maybe memorized them, until there is little to no room for variation. But of course, the minute you bring other people (one or hundreds) into the equation, your well-imagined version of the event disappears. Yet, rigid presenters hold tight to their original plan.

I Don't Have Time to Pay Attention to You

Another source of perceived rigidity is the presenter who is trying to accomplish too much in a limited period of time. If you are very focused on completing your presentation and are driving to a specific goal, you may miss important audience signs of confusion, frustration, or disagreement. An awareness of the subtle and overt reactions of your audience may mean you need to adjust your presentation rather than march onward to the original goal.

Wait, Here Comes the Best Part

Your audience may perceive your delivery as rigid if you do most of the talking. This is often a symptom of having great content; you're excited about the information and want to deliver it well. The trouble comes when you are so focused on wowing them with the details that the presentation becomes a monologue rather than a dialogue. Unless you are a keynote speaker or lecturer, most presentations should be built with multiple "on-ramps" for talking *with* your audience rather than *at* your audience.

Rigid Presenter Examples

It's not possible to show specific examples as easily on these dimensions (versus the example slides in the content and creative sections), but consider the following scenarios and how the presenter responds.

Audience Member:	*That figure doesn't seem right; can we see your math?*
Rigid Presenter:	*The calculations are coming up in two more slides.*
	_____
Relaxed Presenter:	*Sure, let's review that to be sure we're on the same page.*

The original slide order may have seemed logical, but the relaxed presenter recognizes that the audience has to buy-in to the figures to accept his conclusion. The rigid presenter is unwilling to respond to new information.

Audience Member:	*Can we go back and talk more about your auxiliary services?*
Rigid Presenter:	*I'd like to keep going and finish; we can circle back at the end.*
	_____
Relaxed Presenter:	*What aspect would you like to explore further?*

Both presenters are concerned about time and know that a detour may mean they don't get through their planned material. By asking a clarifying question, the relaxed presenter learns more about the audience member and his needs, for example this question may be a "buy signal" and well-worth the detour. The rigid presenter will maintain his schedule, but might miss an opportunity.

67

Audience Member:	*We've only got 10 minutes; can you just hit the highlights?*
Rigid Presenter:	*Perhaps we can reschedule when you have the full hour?*
	———
Relaxed Presenter:	*I'd like to focus on the 3rd agenda point, unless you disagree.*

Asked to reduce an hour in 10 minutes, the rigid presenter tends to give up. He put so much effort into preparing for the meeting he designed that he can't imagine it proceeding any other way. The relaxed presenter takes the change in stride, quickly shifts to the most important issue, and involves the audience in creating a new streamlined agenda.

Audience Member:	*This new "in the cloud" service seems interesting, but is our data safe?*
Rigid Presenter:	*It's absolutely safe.* *[Continues presentation]*
	———
Relaxed Presenter:	*That's a great question, and we spent a lot of time ensuring the data is completely safe. In fact, our CTO just wrote an article about data safety, and I included it in the appendix. I can also arrange for her to call you to discuss.*

The rigid presenter answers accurately, but the relaxed presenter acknowledges the underlying fear and provides two way to address the audience's concern.

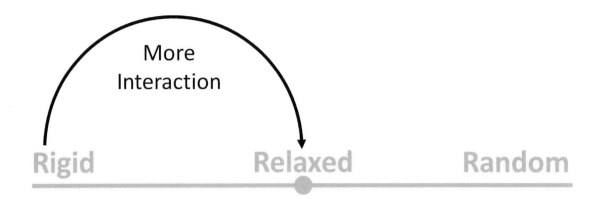

To avoid appearing rigid, create more interaction with your audience. The secret is to <u>plan</u> for <u>choices</u>. Rather than imagining one very specific outcome, imagine a path with many forks. Build contingencies into your presentation, and you won't panic when things don't go exactly as planned. Here are some suggestions:

1. **Offer the People's Choice.** Plan your conversation topics to fit together in many ways and allow your audience to determine the order. This engages the audience and also relaxes you because there is no wrong way to move through the content.

2. **Use Hyperlinks.** If you find that you need to cover topics differently for different audiences, build hyperlinks in your slides (they can be hidden), so that you can quickly move to a topic to deal with a question and then get back to your original slide.

3. **Build in Spacers.** If part of your rigidity is caused by a need to get through a lot of slides in a short time – rethink your content. Make sure to leave at least 10-20% of the meeting time unplanned, so that you can respond to whatever happens.

4. **Listen for Clues.** Your audience will give you signals if you are listening and watching for them. Observe body language and be aware of how questions are phrased to address underlying concerns, confusion, or frustration.

The Random Presenter

Random conversation doesn't necessarily mean you don't *have* a plan, but it does mean you haven't made it clear to your audience. An audience will follow you almost anywhere, as long as you provide maps and milestones along the way. Your style may be perceived as random if you adopt these attitudes:

Spoiler Alert

We all hate when someone blurts out a movie's plot twist or jumps on the punchline of the joke we're telling. Some presenters try to avoid "spoilers" in their presentations. They don't want to "give anything away" and try to keep the key insights of the presentation hidden, so they have the most impact. But unfortunately, that can confuse the audience. The old advice to "tell them what you're going to tell them; tell them; then tell them what you told them" may feel counter-intuitive, but it is effective.

Keep it Real

Some random presenters believe that a lack of preparation creates a more natural exchange with the audience. They avoid rehearsals because they don't want to "sound canned." This approach <u>can</u> work, but only for a specific kind of presenter: a charismatic storyteller. For the rest of us, this approach simply appears unprepared and ineffective. As presenters, we have to *guide the flow* of conversation, and that requires preparation.

Great Question!

Creating an effective conversation with your audience means responding to their questions and concerns, but a random presenter can take this too far. Not all questions should be answered in real-time, but a random presenter sees any question as a passport to explore a new topic. This may be fascinating or frustrating for the audience, but either way, it will not help the meeting reach its desired outcome.

Random Presenter Examples

Consider the random presenter's reaction to our scenarios:

Audience Member:	*That figure doesn't seem right; can we see your math?*
Random Presenter:	*I'm glad you asked– let's rebuild this slide on the white board and confirm each assumption to make sure we agree.*
	_____
Relaxed Presenter:	*Sure, let's review that to be sure we're on the same page.*

The random presenter is always willing to take a conversational off-ramp. In this case, she sees the importance of addressing the audience member's question, but then drifts too far from center by suggesting a time-consuming exercise. If members of the audience share the presenter's penchant for tangents, the meeting can quickly "go down the rabbit hole."

Audience Member:	*Can we go back and talk more about your auxiliary services?*
Random Presenter:	*Absolutely, in addition to these slides, there are case studies in the appendix we can review, too.*
	_____
Relaxed Presenter:	*What aspect would you like to explore further?*

The relaxed presenter uses a follow-up question to understand what's behind the audience member's request. The random presenter jumps on the opportunity to change topics, even introducing additional content. That may be exactly what the audience member wants to know, or the audience member may have had a very quick question. The random presenter doesn't wait to find out.

71

Audience Member:	*We've only got 10 minutes; can you just hit the highlights?*
Random Presenter:	*No Problem*
	[10 minutes later, still on slide2]
	─────
Relaxed Presenter:	*I'd like to focus on the 3rd agenda point, unless you disagree.*

The random presenter is often unaware of his tendency to ramble and weave between topics. He is willing to respond to the request for a short version in theory, but when he starts talking, the conversation controls him.

Audience Member:	*This new "in the cloud" service seems interesting, but is our data safe?*
Random Presenter:	*Let's go to the appendix and review the article from our CTO. You know she also went to Penn State, like you, Steve . . .*
	─────
Relaxed Presenter:	*That's a great question, and we spent a lot of time ensuring the data is completely safe. In fact, our CTO just wrote an article about data safety, and I included it in the appendix. I can also arrange for her to call you to discuss.*

The relaxed presenter offers ways to answer the question outside of the meeting. The random presenter jumps to the new topic, then gets distracted by a personal conversation that might build rapport, but doesn't move the meeting forward.

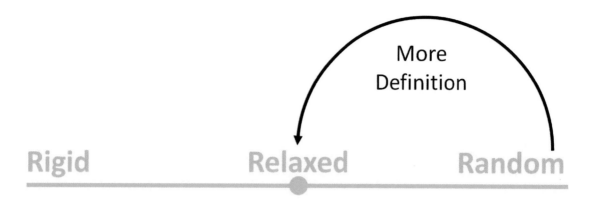

Appearing relaxed requires that you start from a solid plan of approach, but then respond to the needs of a specific audience. Here are some suggestions:

1. **Bake It In.** Include your conversation plan or outline in your presentation. Use an agenda slide or a process diagram to convey "We are here and we're going there" to your audience.

2. **Park It.** Use a parking lot to capture off-topic questions. This can be a simple piece of notebook paper in a small meeting or a flipchart in a large meeting. Never ignore an off-topic question (that's perceived as rigid), but don't allow your conversation to be derailed either.

3. **Get a Stopwatch.** Imagine your client cut your meeting down to five minutes. Right now, present a summary that covers your main points in five minutes. Repeat this exercise until you are certain you know the main points in the most concise order. When you're in the real meeting, let this exercise guide your conversation.

The Relaxed Presenter

Finding a balance in the conversation dimension is about finding a balance between preparation and flexibility. The relaxed presenter has a well thought out plan, yet she is able to respect and *reflect* the needs of the audience in the moment. It is her preparation that gives her the ability to respond to a changing environment and still achieve her goals for the presentation. You can see evidence of a relaxed presenter at several key points in a meeting:

- Meeting Goal/Agenda
- Topic Flow
- Key Points
- Audience Questions
- Off-Topic Discussions
- Presenter Balance
- Content Follows Agenda
- Presentation Timing
- Presenter Inquiries
- Audience Attitude

Meeting Goal/Agenda

When you are presenting at a large conference or meeting, the "conversation" is predominately one-sided. But if you are presenting in a more intimate meeting, you create a dialogue with your audience. And one way to do this is to agree on the meeting goals and agenda.

- **Relaxed**: Presenter checks for agreement and is flexible on agenda and goal
- **Rigid**: Presenter dictates the agenda and states the meeting goal
- **Random**: Presenter makes no effort to establish or agree to agenda or goal

Topic Flow

An audience question or comment may make you realize that there is a better way to present your information. The ability to respond to those in-the-moment changes is a mark of a strong presenter.

- **Relaxed**: Presenter uses plan as a starting point, responds to audience
- **Rigid**: Presenter adheres to plan regardless of external factors
- **Random**: Presenter's plan is missing or vague, topic flow is confusing

Key Points

Your audience will not remember most of what you present. Period.
Knowing this fact, how will you highlight the most important elements?

- **Relaxed**: Key points are highlighted in voice-over and visual elements
- **Rigid**: Key points are given too much attention and repetition
- **Random**: Key points are buried in undifferentiated delivery

Audience Questions

When you engage your audience and challenge their thinking, they will have questions. There's nothing worse than being greeted by silent, blank stares when you ask for questions. We are thankful for interaction and questions. But, can you respond to their questions without derailing your plan?

- **Relaxed**: Questions are encouraged at logical points in the presentation
- **Rigid**: Questions are accepted in the designated Q&A session at the end
- **Random**: Questions are welcomed at any point and answered in great detail

Off-Topic Discussions

An innocent question or remark can take your meeting down an unexpected path. Perhaps you accidentally touched on a sore subject that the team has been working out; perhaps an audience question is so technical that only one person understands or cares about the answer. How do you get the group to return to your meeting without alienating the audience?

- **Relaxed**: Off-topic discussion topics are captured to handle later
- **Rigid**: Off-topic discussions are shut down immediately
- **Random**: Off-topic discussions are welcome and explored in great detail

Presenter Balance

Consider a meeting (not a lecture or keynote address): How much time does the presenter spend speaking versus the group? One of the hallmarks of a conversation is the relative balance of contributions.

- **Relaxed**: Presenter exchanges ideas with the audience and speaks 40-80%
- **Rigid**: Presenter rarely relinquishes "the floor" and speaks +80%
- **Random**: Presenter encourages audience members to jump in at any time and on any topic; presenter speaks <40% of the time

Content Follows Agenda

When you provide an agenda, you set an expectation with your audience. When you follow the agenda, you build their trust. At the same time, your agenda is your best guess of how the meeting should go; the reality of the conversation may require you to be flexible.

- **Relaxed**: Agenda provides a clear plan, with adjustments made based on the flow of the actual meeting conversation
- **Rigid**: Agenda followed exactly; discussion cut short to hit timeline
- **Random**: Any resemblance to an agenda is accidental

Presentation Timing

Gauging the right amount of content to convey your ideas in the time available is a skill that the best presenters acquire through practice. Rehearsal is a key step in preparation to help you estimate your time, but be prepared for the "real thing" to be different than you rehearse. A smart presenter will know in advance where she can cut material to get to the important topics, or how to expand on idea if the meeting time is extended.

- **Relaxed**: Presenter allows 10-20% of time for questions and discussion
- **Rigid**: Presentation fills every minute allotted; presenter's focus is "I have X minutes to say what I need to say" rather than considering what audience needs/wants to hear
- **Random**: Presentation is laughably short (25% of allotted time) or mind-numbingly long (+125% of allotted time)

Presenter Inquiries

In a meeting setting (versus lecture or keynote address), it is effective and appropriate to engage the audience with questions. If you notice the audience is leaning back and just watching, invite them into a conversation. In most cases their body language will change to a more involved, edge-of-the-seat posture.

- **Relaxed**: Presenter asks question to learn about audience needs
- **Rigid**: Presenter asks very few or closed-ended (yes/no) questions
- **Random**: Presenter asks about family and sports (gaining rapport, but not advancing his understanding of the audience's needs)

Audience Attitude

This can be challenging to judge while you are presenting; ask a co-worker to give you feedback. And when you are in an audience, make a mental note of how you and the others are responding to the presenter.

- **Relaxed**: Audience seems engaged, challenged, and involved
- **Rigid**: Audience seems detached, bored, and uninterested
- **Random**: Audience seems confused, bemused, and impatient

Confidence

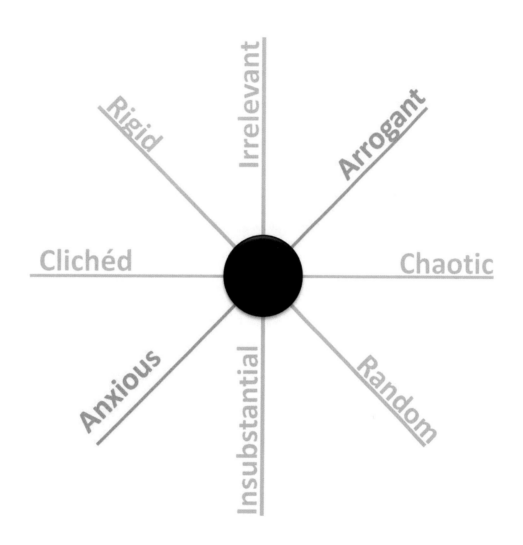

Confidence Dimension

Confidence refers to how the audience perceives you. It can be the most challenging dimension to address, because what feels confident to you may not come across that way to others.

Confidence matters because our audience will use it as a proxy to assess our competence. Think about your own experience as an audience member, how do you access the speaker? Do you believe him? Is he trustworthy? Are you willing to follow his advice? Do you accept his premise? You are gauging all that based on how the speaker moves, talks, and interacts. You are judging him based on his confidence. And he might be surprised by your conclusion.

It can be helpful to recognize that this dimension is about *appearing* confident, not necessarily *being* confident. You don't need years of therapy to improve in this dimension; you need to understand how you are perceived and which behaviors are perceived as confident.

> The desired outcome is to appear confident,
> so the audience is confident in you and your conclusions.

Confidence Definitions

A centered presenter appears _assured_. He knows the material, doesn't get flustered, and accepts challenges and questions from the audience as a mark of their involvement in the presentation.

Anxious   **Assured**   **Arrogant**

When presenters drift from center, they might appear _anxious_. That can include
- someone with "stage fright"
- someone who is uncertain about the material he is presenting
- someone who is too eager to please, too ready to agree with his audience

On the other hand, a presenter who does not establish rapport and who is overly concerned with being perceived as an expert will be perceived as _arrogant_. This perception can also occur when a presenter is very shy; a shy person can seem aloof or detached.

Do you see yourself in this continuum? Consider asking a co-worker or client to provide perceptions on this dimension.

Confidence Quiz

1) Your company uses several acronyms that are uncommon in your industry; you:
   a) Avoid using them at all.
   b) Spell them out the first time used on slide and repeat in definition in your voice-over.
   c) Include the acronyms as needed, assuming the audience will understand through context.

2) What is the best way to connect with your audience?
   a) Rapport – people want to be liked
   b) Empathy – people want to be understood
   c) Logic – people want the facts

3) Do you include callouts of conclusions or key takeaways on your slides?
   a) No, I like to discover what's most important with the specific audience.
   b) Yes, especially on complex graphs or diagrams, I want to be sure we're on the same page.
   c) No, if they don't understand the conclusions, they are not paying attention.

4) At what point in the meeting do you prefer to take questions from your audience?
   a) At any point; it makes the discussion more conversational.
   b) I build in logical places to check for questions. I accept questions at any time; if I know the answer is coming up later in the presentation, I ask them to hold their question.
   c) At the end.

5) Business buzzwords – your take?
   a) I pepper them into my presentation.
   b) I try to be an early adopter on interesting words/phrases, but move on when they become popular.
   c) I rarely use common terms; I employ precise language to eschew obfuscation.

6) You use personal stories in a presentation:
   a) To connect with the audience and make the topics more interesting.
   b) To help the audience see themselves in my solutions.
   c) To demonstrate my experience.

7) The client has asked a complicated question, and you don't feel sure of part of the answer. So:
   a) You speak to the part you know and quickly move on.
   b) You answer the part you know, and then clarify the details for follow-up.
   c) There are no questions you can't answer.

8) If your prospect appears confused about a complex graphic, you
   a) Commiserate and explain you had a hard time with the information from "the bean counters" too.
   b) Try to isolate the point of confusion and find an alternative way to explain the material to make it clearer.
   c) Repeat your explanation verbatim and allow yourself the *tiniest* eye roll when your back is turned.

9) At the end of a client/prospect presentation, do you:
   a) Hope that the conversation leads to next steps.
   b) Suggest next steps for the client/prospect to discuss and confirm.
   c) Include the appropriate next steps, timeline, and assignments.

10) At the end of the presentation, you want your client/prospect to see you as
   a) A friend
   b) A resource
   c) An expert

Scoring

1 point for each A	
5 points for each B	
10 points for each C	
Total Score	

Confidence	Anxious	Assured	Arrogant
	10-35 Points	36-65 Points	66-100 Points
Your Score			

Centering Confidence

Assessing yourself on this dimension is challenging, because it is very personal. It is not about how we <u>are</u>; it is about how we are <u>perceived</u>. It's difficult to be objective about our own confidence level, but there is an immediate reward to addressing a gap in this area, if you have one.

As with the previous dimensions, the go-to response when you feel you're presentation style is not being successful is to do MORE of what feels good to you. And, again, this will lead you further away from being a centered presenter.

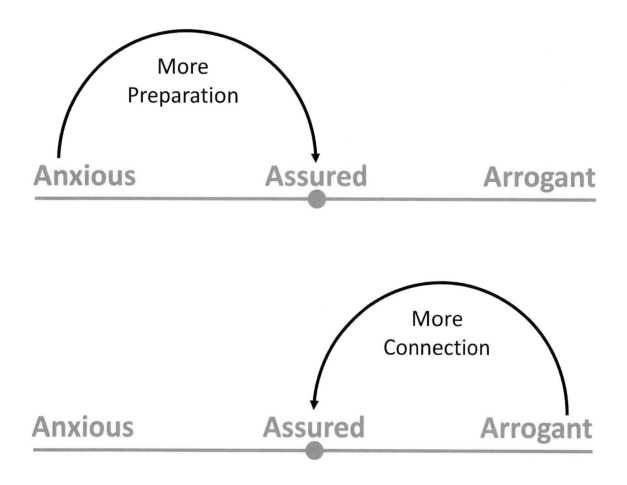

The Anxious Presenter

It may not be fair, but if your audience perceives you as anxious they will often question your competence as well. Several behaviors can make your audience believe you are anxious.

My Hands Always Shake Like This

The good news is, almost everyone in the audience can relate to a *little* nervousness and won't hold it against you. But obvious nerves (shaky hands or voice, flop sweat, etc.) can make your audience uncomfortable or even concerned for your well-being. At that point, they cannot listen to what you are saying.

Is This Distracting? What about This?

Many presenters feel confident and don't have to deal with paralyzing stage fright, yet they still employ a variety of methods to soothe themselves when presenting. Some play with a pen, paper or paperclip; some adjust clothing or jewelry; some use the same word many times without realizing it. Small repetitive gestures can make us feel calmer when we are in a stressful situation. As a presenter you need to use video or trusted feedback to determine if your habits are distracting from your message and making you appear anxious.

The Dog Ate My Speaker Notes

Some presenters sound anxious because they are unprepared. You might have been asked to present at the last minute or you may have simply procrastinated. Whatever the reason - all eyes are on you, and you are not confident in the material or your ability to answer questions. When it comes to reducing presenter anxiety, there is no substitute for solid preparation. You need to work to become comfortable in your subject and your skills. When you are at ease, you put your audience at ease, which means they are ready to listen and consider your ideas.

Anxious Presenter Examples

An anxious presenter may exhibit anxiety, unpreparedness, or stage-fright in a number of ways. Awareness is the first step; you can gain insight through feedback or video. If you see yourself in more than three items listed below, you may have a hard time establishing trust and persuading an audience that you are capable and competent.

Physical Tics

- Adjusting clothing or jewelry
- Jangling change in pocket
- Playing with a pen, rubber band, paperclip, etc
- Stacking and sorting papers
- Gestures that are "too big" for the room or not using any gestures at all and delivering the material in a very stilted manner
- Avoiding eye contact or holding eye contact too long

Verbal Tics

- Filler words like "um" or "ah" or "okay"
- Repeating a particular word in multiple phrases such, as "actually"

Delivery Gaffes

- Upending – making statements sound like questions by raising the pitch at the end of each phrase. (Teenagers tend to do this)
- Monotone – using little or no variation in pitch or speed
- Too fast/slow – nerves can make speakers go to either extreme
- Misspeaking – saying the wrong name for the client or your company, garbling your own product names
- Private comments – adding comments under your breath or when you are turned away from audience
- Standing in your slides – talking in front of the projector so that a portion of the slide is displayed on your face or body

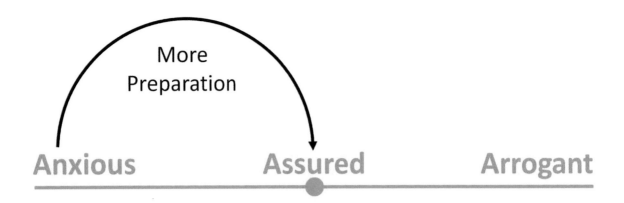

If you feel you are anxious or are perceived as anxious when you present, here are some suggestions:

1. **Don't Try to Fake It.** If you anxiety stems from the fact that you know _only_ the specific information that is on your slides, take the time to talk to experts, review articles, and deepen your understanding.

2. **Practice. A Lot.** Rehearse your presentation itself, but also practice the craft of presenting every chance you get – at work or in social settings. Consider a group like Toastmasters to help you reduce your speaking anxiety and move toward the center with an assured presentation. Watch Ted Talks to see great examples of presentations. [_www.ted.com/talks_]

3. **Silence that Voice in Your Head.** Anxious presenters often focus on that internal critic who judges our every move. That voice is not helping. Stay in the moment.

4. **Shift the Attention.** If your voice or your hand is shaking, give yourself a chance to regain your calm by inviting your audience to expand on an idea or share an experience. When all eyes turn to the new speaker, take a deep breath and re-focus.

The Arrogant Presenter

Very few people set out to appear arrogant; many are not even aware they are perceived as such. When your audience picks up an arrogant vibe, it is usually because they wanted to connect with you but were not able to. Interestingly, there are several root causes that can be perceived as arrogance:

I'm Actually Shy

A shy or introverted presenter can be perceived as arrogant, because they are more comfortable putting a wall between themselves and the audience. If you gravitate to a podium or other physical "shield" you may feel protected, but it is hard to connect with your audience. Many top actors are shy in real life, but appear confident by adopting a public persona; this might work for you.

I'm Actually an Expert

The "arrogant" presenter is sometimes a bona fide expert who lacks the skills or experience to find effective ways to relate her knowledge to her audience. If you fall in this category, your subject matter may feel so natural to you that you forget others need to get up to speed. Enhancing your storytelling skills will help you make your expertise accessible.

I'm Actually Intimidated

A presenter who is intimidated by the situation or audience sometimes tries to counteract this by appearing *aggressively* confident. This is the business equivalent of a peacock spreading its plumage or a rattlesnake shaking its tail. If you find yourself adopting a posture of confidence, your audience may feel that it is not genuine confidence and may not be open to your ideas.

Arrogant Presenter Examples

When we say a presenter seems arrogant, we mean they are attempting to demonstrate that they are **superior** – and whether it is based on legitimate credentials or just an overblown sense of self-worth, it creates a wall between you and the audience. Here are some of the ways arrogance can creep into a presentation.

Body Language
- **Deadpan** – a presenter who never smiles or expresses emotion appears bored or "above" the situation
- **Pointing/Jabbing** – pointing at someone is almost always an aggressive posture; notice that flight attendants always use two fingers
- **Arms crossed** – this posture literally creates a shield in front of your body, suggesting that you are protecting yourself from the audience

Tone of Voice
- **Impatient** – implies that you resent having to "slow down" to answer a question or respond to an audience comment
- **Condescending** – conveys disbelief that you even have to explain this
- **Abrupt** – indicates that you do not welcome interruptions

Word Choice
- **Sesquipedalianism** – the tendency to use long, multi-syllable words when simpler, common words would convey your meaning more clearly
- **Secret Handshake** – using terms or acronyms that only those "in the know" understand
- **Passive Voice** – "The decision was made by the Board…" is an example of passive voice. Compared to the active version ("The Board decided…"), the passive voice appears formal, stilted, and often conveys a nameless authority (e.g. "It was decided that . . .")

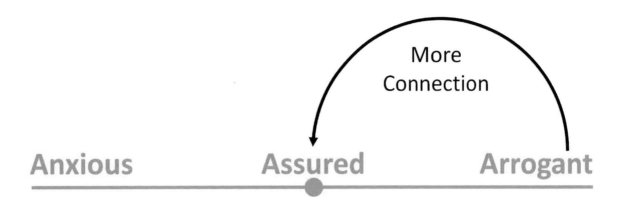

If you are aware that you sometime appear arrogant, shifting back to center requires more connections. Here as some suggestions:

1. **Call Them by Name.** In a small meeting, memorize the attendees. In a large meeting, come a little early and meet a few people. Call on a few audience members by name; it makes a big impression.

2. **Don't Interrupt.** If you are taking questions, don't jump in as soon as you understand the question. Take a moment to appreciate the thought behind the question, even if it is not expressed as clearly as you might like.

3. **Mirror the Question.** Rather than answer right away, rephrase "So your question is . . ." This makes the person asking the question feel heard and also ensures you are answering the right question.

4. **Play the Fool.** If you are a potentially intimidating expert, or your anecdotes tend to focus on what you've accomplished and who you know, try sharing a story where you look just a *little* foolish. Your audience will relate to you and be more open to your expertise.

5. **Have a Seat**. If you are physically imposing (e.g., tall), try presenting while seated at least part of the time to maintain a more casual connection.

The Assured Presenter

Confidence is hard to define and can look very different on different people; yet we know it when we see it. Feedback from others or a video of yourself can be invaluable in identifying and addressing issues on this continuum. Keep in mind that what <u>feels</u> confident on the inside can appear distracting or distancing on the outside. Practice observing other presenters to gain insight into the attributes of this dimension.

- Facial Expression
- Sentence Structure
- Voice (when presenting)
- Voice (when answering)
- Use of Humor
- Movement
- Gestures
- Technical Difficulties
- Audience Rapport
- Perceived Expertise

Facial Expression

The next time you are in a public place, such as an airport, glance at the faces of strangers and notice how quickly you get a "gut feeling" about them. Do they seem approachable? Distracted? Angry? Scared? Your instant analysis may not be <u>right</u>, but you will quickly categorize them. We do this subconsciously every time we meet a new person. Your audience will do it, too - before you utter your first word. The expression on your face is their first clue about your level of confidence. Remember, the best speakers <u>do</u> feel a little nervous, but they don't show it.

- **Assured**: A relaxed, open expression; more likely to "smile with his eyes" than with a toothy grin; jaw is relaxed, teeth slightly apart; meets the gaze of the audience
- **Anxious**: A pinched, closed expression; eyes down or on paperwork; tension will manifest in various ways such as clenched jaw, tight neck, flushed skin, perspiration, wide eyes, or a tight smile
- **Arrogant**: A bored or proud expression; may appear contemptuous of the room, the event, or the audience; looks through the audience

Sentence Structure

Notice as you observe other presenters how their words and ideas flow. Do they struggle to form coherent sentences; do they change ideas midstream? Or do they tend to make pronouncements rather than engage in conversation? How you order your sentences is another clue about your confidence.

- **Assured**: Active voice ("We decided."); owns his ideas and actions; short sentences that are easy to understand and follow
- **Anxious**: Disjointed; a lot of starts and stops; filled with verbal stops ("um")
- **Arrogant**: Passive voice ("It was decided."); convoluted sentences that may be brilliant but are very difficult to comprehend; stilted, formal style

Voice (when presenting)

Presenting is different than just talking with a group; presenting is similar to performing. You need to capture and hold the audience's attention with the ideas you present, your physical presence, and the tone of your voice.

- **Assured**: Speaks in a tone that is loud enough for the room, with clear articulation and a friendly tone of voice
- **Anxious**: Speaks softly or drops the volume at ends of phrases; mumbles
- **Arrogant**: Speaks slightly too loudly, uses a pompous tone of voice that seems bored, superior, or sarcastic

Voice (when answering)

When interacting with your audience, you should adopt a more conversational tone, but you still need to be loud enough for all participants to understand the question and your response.

- **Assured**: Respectful, repeats the question (if appropriate) and answers so that everyone can benefit from the exchange
- **Anxious**: Uncertain, forgets to answer for the larger group
- **Arrogant**: Impatience, sarcasm or contempt may creep into the response

Use of Humor

We're not talking about old school ". . . and boy, are my arms tired" jokes. Instead, consider how a sense of fun can lighten your presentation and engage the audience. No one is expecting a comedy routine, but a few humorous moments will increase rapport and help your audience remember you.

- **Assured**: Light touches of humor or wordplay
- **Anxious**: Attempts at self-deprecating humor that tend to result in awkward silence from audience
- **Arrogant**: Mocking humor that is actually a camouflaged insult

Movement

If you think of the presentation as a kind of performance, you begin to understand why movement is an integral concept. As you walk, you use large muscles which can reduce tension – helping to relieve nervousness.

- **Assured**: Moves easily about the room, stops to deliver next point
- **Anxious**: Rarely moves, paces, or stands *in* the projected slides
- **Arrogant**: Rooted to podium as authority position

Gestures

Our hands are with us all the time, but sometimes when we get up to present, we completely forget what to do with them. Observe strong presenters; notice that they are comfortable with their arms and hands in a neutral position much of the time. They use gestures to augment their message.

- **Assured**: Uses gestures to support ideas and enhance storytelling
- **Anxious**: Holds arms stiffly with little or no gesturing; or flails wildly
- **Arrogant**: Stiff, repetitive gestures, often with pointing/accusing fingers

Technical Difficulties

The cord you left at home, the projector that won't turn on, the room that is 20 degrees too warm – the list of things that can (and will) go wrong is long. We've all been there and can relate. So can your audience. The question is: how will you deal with it?

- **Assured**: Adjusts; uses a "plan B" approach to convey information
- **Anxious**: Panics; becomes obsessed with making the original plan work
- **Arrogant**: Complains; blames others and expects "someone" to fix it

Audience Rapport

Some people think rapport is when the audience likes the presenter. I would argue it is when the presenter likes the *audience*.

- **Assured**: Creates undeniable rapport with sincere interest in audience
- **Anxious**: Unable to establish rapport; thinks audience is not interest**ed**
- **Arrogant**: Unwilling to establish rapport; thinks audience is not interest**ing**

Perceived Expertise

It may not be fair or accurate, but your confidence level is used as a proxy for your competence level.

- **Assured**: Presenter is perceived as competent in her field
- **Anxious**: Presenter is interpreted as incompetent
- **Arrogant**: Presenter is seen as intimidating or overcompensating

Presenter Assessment

Use this assessment while reviewing a video of yourself giving a presentation, or ask for feedback from a co-worker. Circle the behaviors that apply:

Conversation	Rigid	Relax	Random
Meeting Goal / Agenda	Dictates	Collaborates	Ignores
Topic Flow	Linear	Organic	Confusing
Key Points	Over-Emphasized	Highlighted	Buried
Audience Questions	Only at End	At Logical Stops	At Any Point
Off-Topic Discussions	Not Tolerated	Captured for Later	Welcome
Presenter Balance	> 80%	40% - 80%	< 40%
Content Follows Agenda	Exactly	Effectively	Accidentally
Presentation Timing	Fills Every Minute	Room for Discussion	Too Long or Short
Presenter Inquiries	Few Questions	About Needs	About Family
Audience Attitude	Detached	Engaged	Confused
Score			

Confidence	Anxious	Assured	Arrogant
Facial Expression	Pinched / Sweaty	Open / Friendly	Closed / Bored
Sentence Structure	Awkward	Active Voice	Passive Voice
Voice (when presenting)	Quiet / Weak	Clear / Confident	Loud / Pompous
Voice (when answering)	Uncertain	Respectful	Impatient
Use of Humor	Self-Deprecating	Light / Appropriate	Mocking
Movement	Stands in Slides	Moves around Room	Podium / One Spot
Gestures	Missing or Wild	Supports Ideas	Stiff / Accusing
Technical Difficulties	Panics	Adjusts	Complains
Audience Rapport	Unable	Undeniable	Unwilling
Perceived Expertise	Incompetent	Competent	Intimidating
Score			

Top three items to address:

1.

2.

3.

Where do you see yourself as a presenter on the chart below?

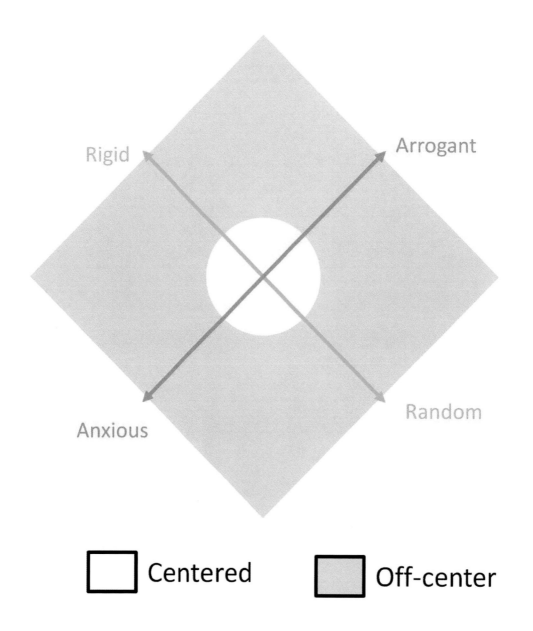

Rigid

Arrogant

Anxious

Random

□ Centered   ▨ Off-center

Are you drifting from center?

Where do others see you?

Conversation
& Confidence

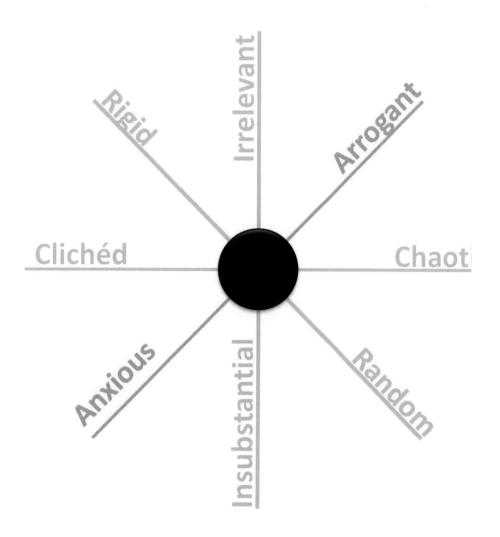

The Intersection of
Conversation and Confidence

Earlier we looked at the intersection of two dimensions of centered presentations that are about the presentation itself: **CONTENT** and **CREATIVE**. Now let's consider the two that focus on the presenter: CONVERSATION and CONFIDENCE.

A centered presenter engages in relaxed conversation and is perceived as assured. His approach to the presentation connects him to the audience and to his topic. He is an **influencer**.

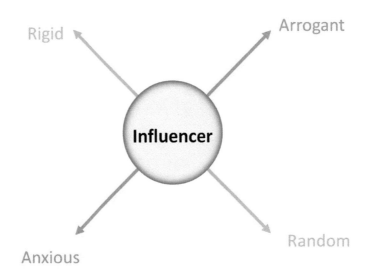

How do these dimensions combine when there are issues of both conversation and confidence?

The Imposter

When a presenter appears anxious or uncertain and is also tied to a very rigid conversational style, the audience perceives him as an **imposter**. They may assume the "real" presenter was called away - leaving them with the B-team.

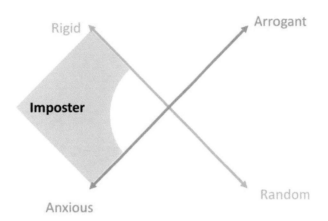

Move toward the center with more preparation before and more interaction during your meeting. If your presentation style drifts from the center into this quadrant, use the checklist below.

- ☐ Focus on the desired outcome of the meeting, not the schedule
- ☐ Imagine four different paths that could reach the same outcome
- ☐ Rehearse with an "audience" that makes you go off-script
- ☐ Use a "parking lot" to be sure the audience feels heard even if you delay answering a question
- ☐ Build in buffer time so you are not derailed by questions

- ☐ Identify your nervous tics and practice (often!) to reduce them
- ☐ Before you present, privately repeat your 3-5 key points without looking at slides
- ☐ Establish a subtle signal for your co-worker to comment on a question
- ☐ Rehearse with an "audience" that challenges and interrupts
- ☐ Visualize the meeting in advance; see yourself succeeding

The Bungler

A presenter whose confidence level is low and who presents topics in a seemingly random fashion is perceived as a fool or a **bungler**. The audience may be sympathetic at first, but they will quickly become irritated that their time is being wasted.

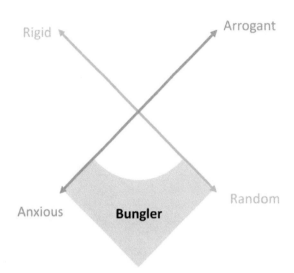

Change the perception by combining better preparation with more defined conversation flow; consider the checklist below.

- ☐ Establish and share an agenda for every presentation
- ☐ Use "you are here" graphics to help the audience follow your flow
- ☐ Rehearse with an "audience" that tries to distract you
- ☐ Use a "parking lot" to capture stray ideas but not spend time on them
- ☐ Summarize your key ideas at the end; aligned with the agenda and stated goal for the meeting

- ☐ Identify your nervous tics and practice (often!) to reduce them
- ☐ Before you present, privately repeat your 3-5 key points without looking at slides
- ☐ Establish a subtle signal for your co-worker to comment on a question
- ☐ Rehearse with an "audience" that challenges and interrupts
- ☐ Visualize the meeting in advance; see yourself succeeding

The Stickler

Combine a tendency toward arrogance with a rigid adherence to a conversation plan, and you have a presenter who's perceived as a **stickler**. This presenter is very literal and focuses so much on minute details that the big picture can be lost.

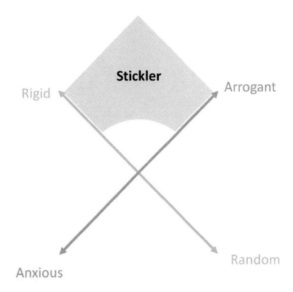

Focusing on the audience, making more connections and having more interactions will return this presenter to the center.

- ☐ Focus on the desired outcome of the meeting not the schedule
- ☐ Imagine four different paths that could reach the same outcome
- ☐ Rehearse with an "audience" that makes you go off-script
- ☐ Use a "parking lot" to be sure the audience feels heard even if you delay answering a question
- ☐ Build in buffer time so you are not derailed by questions

- ☐ Identify your arrogant habits and practice (often!) to reduce them
- ☐ Eliminate passive voice from your presentation
- ☐ Recognize you can learn something from your audience every time
- ☐ Rehearse with an "audience" that asks obvious questions; answer with respect and patience
- ☐ Sit down for part of the meeting; be on the same level, less formal

The Strutter

The final combination is a presenter who is perceived as overly confident but who communicates in a random fashion. Like an absent-minded professor spouting random theories for his class, this presenter appears pompous and detached.

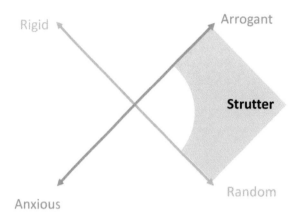

Add definition to the conversation to bring the audience with you and find ways to make more connections.

☐ Establish and share an agenda for every presentation

☐ Use "you are here" graphics to help the audience follow your flow

☐ Rehearse with an "audience" that tries to distract you

☐ Use a "parking lot" to capture stray ideas but not spend time on them

☐ Summarize your key ideas at the end; aligned with the agenda and stated goal for the meeting

☐ Identify your arrogant habits and practice (often!) to reduce them

☐ Eliminate passive voice from your presentation

☐ Recognize you can learn something from your audience every time

☐ Rehearse with an "audience" that asks obvious questions; answer with respect and patience

☐ Sit down for part of the meeting; be on the same level, less formal

Centered Presentation Summary

If you are not happy with your presentations, first consider if the issue is with the material or the delivery.

Should you focus on **CONTENT** and **CREATIVE**? Or is it more appropriate to work on CONVERSATION and CONFIDENCE?

Remember that if you are adrift on any of these dimensions you need to get back to the center, even though it may feel comfortable to you to do more of what you're good at. Instead do more of what balances your natural tendency.

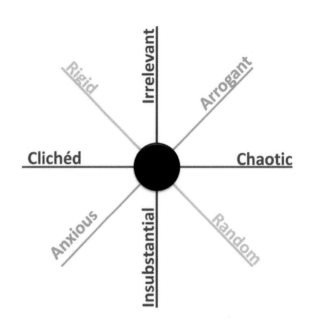

Insubstantial Content ....More Proof

Irrelevant Content ....More Editing

Clichéd Creative...More Variety

Chaotic Creative ....More Structure

Rigid Conversation.....................................More Interaction

Random Conversation ....More Definition

Anxious ....More Preparation

Arrogant ....More Connection

Centering Your Team
or Yourself

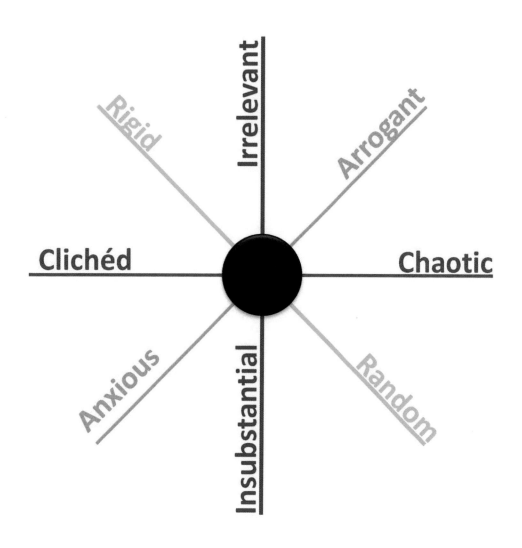

Centering Your Team or Yourself

A new presentation needs to be created; how do you begin? Many of us have been guilty of simply firing up PowerPoint and starting to type. We know the name and date of the meeting, so BOOM, first slide is done. Feels like we're making progress, right? A few slides in, we might feel a little lost, but we press on, leaving placeholders for content that will come from other team members. When their slides arrive, they don't quite gel with the content we created – but now the meeting is tomorrow, so we force it to fit.

Can you relate?

Now imagine a slightly different approach, an approach that provides clarity to the development of content; an approach that gives context to the creative plan. All team members working on the content have a clear understanding of what should be included and how the presentation should look and feel. Like a Hollywood movie "shot out of sequence," content developers focus attention on the topics that are most important to the audience, rather than starting on page one and forging ahead.

The keys to this approach: investing more time in planning/discussion before you start a presentation and documenting important aspects of the presentation in a Content Brief and a Creative Brief.

Content Brief

It doesn't take a lot of time to provide content clarity, but it does take a commitment to creating a content brief by answering (or reaching consensus on) questions that provide the foundation for content development.

- What type of presentation is this?
- What is the desired outcome of this presentation?
- What are the obstacles to that outcome?
- What tools will be used to overcome each obstacle?
- What are the main topics of this presentation?
- What is the planned flow and proportion of these topics and why?
- Who are the decision makers in the audience?
- Where are the decision-makers on the buy cycle?
- If the audience remembers one thing, what should that be?
- What are the presentation logistics?

What type of presentation is this?

In broad terms, business presentations can be categorized based on their purpose: Educate, Explore, Negotiate, or Convert

- A meeting designed to **educate** will be more straight-forward, and you will present almost as a monologue.
  Your tone will "**tell**"

- A meeting designed to **explore** will include more questions, will solicit feedback, and will create a dialogue.
  Your tone will "**ask**"

- A meeting designed to **negotiate** is appropriate when it's not a question of if your prospect will buy, but if he will buy from you.
  Your tone will "**sell**"

- A meeting designed to convert is used to change your audience's mind. In sales this is when your prospect already buys your product or service from another provider and you want to unseat the incumbent. In a non-sales meeting, it is when the *idea* you are presenting (selling!) is very different than the audience's perception.
  Your tone will "**compel**"

When you identify your presentation type, you create a filter for the content and tone of the presentation.

What is the desired outcome of this presentation?

Fast-forward to the end of the meeting, what do you want your audience to do? Agree to the next meeting? Introduce you to higher level executives? Sign on the dotted line? Be very clear about the goal for this meeting – and the meeting goal may be different from your overarching goal. For example, even if you are hoping to sell $10M to Acme Inc, the goal for your next meeting may be to have the key executives agree to tour your plant. The more concrete your presentation goal, the better. And please identify only one desired outcome. Don't dilute your focus with a laundry list.

What are the obstacles to that outcome?

Put yourself in your audience's mind. What will stop the desired next step? Is your audience:

- Skeptical of the claims in the presentation?
- Confused by technical jargon or diagrams?
- Loyal to a current provider?
- Concerned about the effort needed to go with a new solution?
- Unsure this idea can be sold internally to her superiors?
- Simply comfortable with the status quo?

What tools will be used to overcome each obstacle?

For each obstacle, overtly describe how your presentation will address and, hopefully, overcome the issue. For example, if you think your audience will be skeptical, make it a priority to include footnoted sources, laboratory reports, client testimonials, or other proof points that strengthen your claims. If you think your audience will not want to invest the time to make a change (e.g., bring on a new vendor), then demonstrate the simple, proven process your company provides to remove or reduce the risk during transition.

The answer will be unique to your situation, but by identifying the potential issues and an approach to overcome each, you have highlighted key areas that can be woven into the entire presentation.

What are the main topics of this presentation?

Describing the components of your content is very helpful in planning, but many people find this step difficult. They either drop down to a very granular level of dozens of points they want to cover, or they repeat the presentation title as one big topic. Identifying 3-5 topics will clarify your thinking and also provide a filter to remove content that does not belong in this presentation.

What is the planned flow and proportion of these topics and why?

This answer is subject to change as you begin to build the presentation, but it's vital to start with a rough plan for your main topics. How do you see the sequence of the presentation and how much time and material belongs in each section?

Who are the decision-makers in the audience?

Whether you are working alone or with a team, it's helpful to consider who will be in the room for your presentation. Even in the case of a broad audience, e.g., a session at a convention with hundreds of participants, think about the roles in the audience and who would have authority to follow-up with you.

Where are the decision-makers on the buy cycle?

There are several versions of the classic buy cycle, but most are similar to:

Awareness – Consideration – Decision – Purchase – Repurchase

The idea is that as we move through the cycle we need different information and are open (or resistant) to different ideas. Think of the classic used car salesman, trying to force a "hard sell" on someone who is merely toying with the idea of buying a car. That's a caricature, but it is rooted in truth: if we ignore the buy cycle, we risk alienating our prospect.

Note: Even if your presentations are not sales presentations in the literal sense, you are selling ideas and asking your audience to "buy" them.

If the audience remembers one thing, what should that be?

Research has shown that there is a precipitous drop-off in what we remember after 24, 48, and 72 hours. Your audience <u>will</u> forget most of what you present. Knowing this, if there is one idea they will remember: what should it be?

Now, how can you weave that element into your presentation so that it is reinforced and memorable? Repetition helps, as does expressing the idea through multiple methods: words on the slide, in your voice over, or in graphics.

What are the presentation logistics?

What are the details you must remember when building your content? This is especially important if the presenter is not the one developing content; make certain his or her preferences and expectations are clarified.

- Time, date, and location
- Client or audience
- Type of audience: client, prospect, public, internal, etc
- How much time is dedicated to the presentation?
- How big is the room?
- Will the presentation be projected or printed?
- Does a separate leave-behind document need to be built, perhaps with black & white images and fewer pages?
- What internal research or reports should be reflected?
- Is there secondary research required, and if so, for what proof points?
- Does the presenter want to be able to jump through the presentation with hyperlinks?
- Does the presenter have a preference about slide animation and/or slide transitions?
- Does the presenter need/want a "speaker's notes" version with additional detail (especially helpful if multiple members are developing content)

Content Brief - Sample

What type of presentation is this?	☐ Educate (tell) ☐ Explore (ask) ☑ Negotiate (sell) ☐ Convert (compel)
What is the desired outcome of this presentation?	Prospect will commit to exhibit at next year's convention
What are the obstacles to that outcome?	A. Expense/Time B. Skeptical of quality of convention attendees
What tools will be used to overcome each obstacle?	A. Menu of options to control exhibitor expense A. Average ROI of last year's exhibitors B. Last year's roster B. Attendee survey results and quotes
What are the main topics of this presentation?	Convention Overview Exhibitor Benefits Exhibitor Tools
What is the planned flow and proportion of these topics and why?	Convention Overview – 15% Exhibitor Benefits – 40% Exhibitor Tools – 45% Why: demonstrate how easy it is to add to convention calendar and that benefits outweigh expense
Who are the decision makers in the audience?	Fred Jones, CMO Sara Grant, Convention Director
Where are the decision makers on the buy cycle?	☐ Awareness ☐ Consideration ☑ Decision ☐ Purchase ☐ Repurchase They are finalizing the next 18 months; ready to commit
If the audience remembers one thing, what should that be?	Our convention serves a unique niche and offers cost-effective access to their prospect base
What are the presentation logistics?	• Prospect meeting on 4/13 at Acme offices in New York • Will present from printed slides in office setting • Limit use of builds; print builds on separate slides if used • Create a PDF version for iPad use as well

Content Brief Template

What type of presentation is this?	☐ Educate (tell) ☐ Explore (ask) ☐ Negotiate (sell) ☐ Convert (compel)
What is the desired outcome of this presentation?	
What are the obstacles to that outcome?	
What tools will be used to overcome each obstacle?	
What are the main topics of this presentation?	
What is the planned flow and proportion of these topics and why?	
Who are the decision makers in the audience?	
Where are the decision makers on the buy cycle?	☐ Awareness ☐ Consideration ☐ Decision ☐ Purchase ☐ Repurchase
If the audience remembers one thing, what should that be?	
What are the presentation logistics?	

Creative Brief

You may know that graphic artists and marketing agencies require creative briefs from their clients. In fact, most won't begin work without one.

Whether you are working alone or with a team, what if you took the time to write out a brief for your presentation creative? It does not take that long (hey, that's why it's called a "brief"). This powerful tool will force you to spell out your goals for the presentation and how you envision the creative supporting your message.

It will literally *center* your thinking.

As with the Content Brief, it's helpful to complete the Creative Brief *as if you were going to assign the creative aspects to your presentation to someone else (whether you are or not)*. Spell out the details as clearly as you can. Use your answers as a filter and guide as you work on or review your creative.

- Details
- Audience Target
- Presentation Lifecycle
- Library
- Key Milestones and Timing
- Presentation Purpose
- Presentation Tone
- Brand Mandatories
- Presentation Style
- Audience Current State
- Audience Desired State
- Other Notes

Details

Provide the company name, meeting location, meeting date, meeting name

Audience Target

Confirm that the audience will be comprised of clients, prospects, the general public, an internal group, etc.

Presentation Lifecycle

Set an expectation for the presentation itself; do you see this as a one-time presentation or will it be repurposed and reused in future situations? Knowing that you are creating a presentation that will have a longer "shelf life" can justify spending more time on graphic elements or building true templates so that it can be easily repurposed for another client, for example.

Library

Provide guidance on any reference materials or templates that can be used for this presentation. Does this presentation need to have similar look and feel to existing materials? Is it part of a "library" of materials that can be used to speed development?

Key Milestones and Timing

Again, whether you are working alone or delegating to a team, establish internal deadlines for review, rehearsal, proofreading etc. This allows you to better manage time and avoid panic.

Presentation Purpose

Give context, especially if the team working on creative was not involved in content development. You can also attach the Content Brief for reference.

Presentation Tone

How do you want to be perceived? For example: formal, informal, serious, humorous, playful, excited, apologetic, or educational. When you have a filter for tone, it is easier to identify and correct slides that are "out of character" for your presentation.

Brand Mandatories

These are requirements from the prospect or client (as opposed to your internal brand guidelines.) Provide specific requirements for logo, color, etc.

Presentation Style

This is especially helpful if working with a team. Create a shared vocabulary and shorthand to describe different creative styles. You can add or modify the categories below; you might also provide examples for new members of the team to see "what a 7 looks like."

Scale of 1-10

_____Text: sparse (1) to dense (10)
_____Graphics: decorative (1) to integrated (10)
_____Colors: minimal (1) to vibrant (10)
_____Animation: none (1) to complex (10)
_____Transitions: none (1) to every slide (10)

Audience Current State

Although creative is made up of technical choices (like color, font, graphics), the creative is also a vehicle to touch the emotions of the audience. Share any insight you have about the audience current state; what are they bringing to the meeting? Any baggage? You might describe the current state as closed, open, intrigued, angry, doubtful, curious, distracted, bored, resentful, etc.

Audience Desired State

How you want them to feel AFTER presentation: convinced, open to further discussion, reassured, intrigued, satisfied, hungry for next steps, etc.

Other Notes

Any additional elements needed, such as posters, handouts, etc.? Include any other facts or requirements that will inform creative development.

A Sample Creative Brief

Details	Acme Inc – Quarterly Review Meeting 9/1 Acme Headquarters boardroom
Audience Target	3-5 marketing staff members, including CMO CFO has been invited but may not attend
Presentation Lifecycle	Would like to create a template that can be re-used each quarter but still allow variation to feel fresh
Library	Should be consistent with other Acme presentations
Key Milestones and Timing	First internal review 8/17; Rehearsal 8/25
Presentation Purpose	High level of overview of quarterly performance with illustrative charts on key performance indicators; slides should highlight "so what" of data presented
Presentation Tone	Confident, conversational, but not overly familiar
Brand Mandatories	Acme logo must appear in lower left of all slides and handouts
Presentation Style	Scale of 1-10 __5__ Text: sparse (1) to dense (10) __7__ Graphics: decorative (1) to integrated (10) __3__ Colors: minimal (1) to vibrant (10) __2__ Animation: none (1) to complex (10) __1__ Transitions: none (1) to every slide (10)
Audience Current State	Slightly annoyed by last month's shipping delay; generally positive attitude
Audience Desired State	Convinced that we have solved shipping issue and confident in our plans for next quarter
Other Notes	The CFO hates 3D charts; use 2D

Creative Brief Form

Details	
Audience Target	
Presentation Lifecycle	
Library	
Key Milestones and Timing	
Presentation Purpose	
Presentation Tone	
Brand Mandatories	
Presentation Style	Scale of 1-10 _____Text: sparse (1) to dense (10) _____Graphics: decorative (1) to integrated (10) _____Colors: minimal (1) to vibrant (10) _____Animation: none (1) to complex (10) _____Transitions: none (1) to every slide (10)
Audience Current State	
Audience Desired State	
Other Notes	

About Jennifer Palus

For more than twenty-five years, I've worked to create the infrastructure, process, and packaging that make a proposal or presentation sing. Whether partnering directly with a client or with an internal colleague or team, I have had the privilege to work with thought leaders who want to elevate deliverables in terms of format, flow, and strategic content.

My career spans a variety of industries, including retail, wholesale distribution, consumer goods, financial services, and consulting. My specific areas of expertise include strategic planning, trend analysis, data management, business intelligence, and marketing communications.

If you enjoyed this book, I hope you'll visit my website:

www.palusbusinessconsulting.com

Learn more about my services:
- Professional storytelling: Distilling your message to its essence
- Presentation development and delivery skills
- Customized training for Microsoft Office; Word, Excel, PowerPoint
- Meeting facilitation
- Training design, documentation, and facilitation
- Project planning and management

Made in the USA
Lexington, KY
21 December 2013